A TRUE STORY OF

BORN

OVERCOMING SAME-SEX ATTRACTION

THAT

WITH INSIGHTS FOR FRIENDS,

WAY?

FAMILIES, AND LEADERS

ERIN ELDRIDGE

Deseret Book Company
Salt Lake City, Utah

Library of Congress Cataloging-in-Publication Data

Eldridge, Erin.
  Born that way? : a true story of overcoming same-sex attraction /
Erin Eldridge.
    p.   cm.
  ISBN 0–87579–835–7
  1. Lesbianism—Religious aspects—Mormon Church—Case studies.
2. Substance abuse—Religious aspects—Christianity—Case studies.
3. Eldridge, Erin. 4. Mormon Church—Doctrines. 5. Church of Jesus
Christ of Latter-day Saints—Doctrines. 6. Repentance—Mormon
Church—Case studies. 7. Forgiveness of sin—Case studies.
8. Spiritual healing—Case studies. I. Title
BX8643.L55E75   1994
261.8'357663—dc20   93–48687
                                                                                    CIP

Printed in the United States of America
10 9   8   7   6   5   4   3   2   1

CONTENTS

PREFACE

Back when I was struggling to gain freedom from same-sex attraction, I could not find any books written by members of the LDS Church who had dealt with the issue. Angrily I would insist, "'The Church' doesn't understand. 'They' don't even care enough to write a book on homosexuality."

By the time I brought my life into harmony with the gospel, however, I had realized the Church was not "they." And perhaps the "they" I was criticizing included the "I" who should quit complaining and start writing. So I did.

Actual names and some details have been changed or withheld to preserve privacy. Maybe the day will come when that will not be necessary.

I have researched same-sex attraction extensively, but I do not claim to be an expert on the subject. My greatest knowledge comes from having lived through it. I incorporate what I've learned through the Spirit, and from inspired friends, my own experiences, and the struggles of those with whom I counsel nonprofessionally.

Experience has been a powerful catalyst as well as an exacting teacher. The memory of my own desperate struggle provided me with the motivation to begin and then continue writing this book in an effort to give hope to those who face challenges similar to mine.

CHAPTER 1

LOBSTER BOY

Several years ago I attended the state fair. It had the usual Ferris wheels and roller coasters, fun houses and merry-go-rounds. Cotton candy was strewn from one end to the other.

But along the back side of the fairgrounds was a row of trailers with plywood walls in front of them. They were painted with pictures and banners that read "The Two-Headed Maiden," "Bearded Lady," and "Hercules." I figured it was all a big farce, but curiosity got me to spend the fifty cents to see "Lobster Boy." I fully expected to find some kid sitting in a tub full of lobsters or some poorly retouched photograph combining a lobster and a human.

What I did not expect to find was a real live man, a dwarf, sitting there with his shoes off. He was crippled, and his legs and feet were badly deformed. Each foot had a warped big toe with a second toe that curled in towards it. (I guess that's where they got the lobster part.) His wife, or a friend, was sitting there holding his hand, almost as if she were there to comfort him through the ordeal.

I was mortified. Not because of how he looked but because I had just paid to walk in and see this poor man. I couldn't get out fast enough. There was a crowd of people on both sides. Kids were pointing and laughing. It was like a bad dream.

The experience deeply upset me. Later I realized it was more than just being troubled by the poor man's condition and my having contributed to it, as if that weren't bad enough. But what really disturbed me was the realization that I felt just like Lobster Boy. I was the "freak in the sideshow."

Like my first day back in church after years of inactivity and years of homosexual activity. There I was in the back row. The freak. The oddball. The misfit. The queer. I felt I should put up a sign and charge admission.

Of course, no one there knew. But boy if they had, I was sure they would have pointed and laughed.

Many who live a homosexual life have faced public persecution. Yet Christ asks us not to judge others, including those who live a homosexual life.

I do not stand in judgment now. I realize not everyone considers same-sex attraction to be a trial or a struggle. This book is intended for those who believe that The Church of Jesus Christ of Latter-day Saints is true. It is for those who believe, somewhere deep within, that homosexual behavior is sin and should be overcome. This book cannot change minds and does not attempt to. But for those who are earnestly seeking, it is my hope this book can help change lives.

It is also my hope to bring a greater understanding of this issue to other Church members, so together we can create a haven where those trying to leave homosexual relationships can come for help. This is the Church of Jesus Christ, and it is Christlike love, fellowship, and acceptance that will help bring healing. There can be no pointing or laughing or collecting of tickets.

Many mistakenly believe that those who struggle with homosexual desires asked or wanted or even consciously chose to have such feelings. Although we are not certain of the causes, we do know that, in most cases, same-sex attraction is not chosen.

Many who struggle to find freedom from homosexual desires believe they must spend the rest of their lives in constant turmoil. That is also a misperception. Although there are still many questions concerning the causes of same-sex attraction, Christ provides the solution.

One of the latest trends in scientific research has been directed toward finding biological and genetic links to homosexual inclinations. Many are now saying that homosexually oriented people are "born that way." From a religious perspective, some insist that if there is a genetic link—if by nature people are born with homosexual tendencies—then God must approve.

The definition of repentance in the Bible Dictionary states that "since we are born into conditions of mortality, repentance comes to mean . . . a renunciation of sin to which we are *naturally inclined*." (Emphasis added.) It is possible that homosexual inclinations may, in fact, be natural inclinations for some, but that does not make it spiritually correct to act on those tendencies.

We are each inclined to sin. We are all born human and have a fallen nature. "And Satan came among them. . . . And men began from that time forth to be carnal, sensual, and devilish." (Moses 5:13.) Our carnal and sensual desires differ, but we all have them. We are all "born that way," born with tendencies to commit a variety of sins. Yet God still asks us to overcome. That is the test of mortality.

The statement "born that way" can also imply "once a homosexual, always a homosexual." That is not true. There are private and public stories of people who have found freedom from homosexual desires. Even those who never had any attractions toward the opposite sex while growing up have discovered such attractions later, usually after abandoning homosexual relationships and working through feelings.

This is not to imply that all who leave a homosexual life will find a person of the opposite sex they wish to marry. Not everyone, whatever their circumstance, is promised the opportunity of eternal marriage in this life. But Christ does promise each of us the opportunity to gain freedom from sin and from the overwhelming desire to sin.

Many promote a limited view of change, insisting it is impossible for a "homosexual" to become a "heterosexual." Christ offers us a greater, all-encompassing transformation—the mighty change of heart, or being born of God. It is the change from desiring to do those things that are not in accordance with God's will to desiring to do those things that are.

The emphasis of this book is on gaining freedom from same-sex attraction. By this I mean that individuals can abstain from sexual relationships with others of the same sex, overcome such desires, and cease to consider themselves homosexual.

In the next chapter I relate my own story. Then the following chapter, "Am I Gay?" discusses some possible biological and environmental causes of same-sex attraction. In that chapter I also address the concept that homosexual behavior is sinful. I do so in an effort to help those who waiver—who believe on a strong day that such behavior is sin but find themselves rationalizing their behavior on a weak day.

The subsequent chapters discuss what I have learned about hope, faith, charity, repentance, baptism, the sacrament, and the mighty change, and how these principles and ordinances of the gospel related to my process of overcoming. But these principles did not work, nor can they work, isolated from the others. And each chapter involves something of a retelling of parts of my story to illustrate my growth over the years with regard to each precept. I describe my progression from darkness to the light of hope, from doubt to faith and the power to overcome, from loneliness to being filled with charity, and from feeling overwhelmed by unrighteous desires to completely turning my will over to God.

Gospel principles apply to my struggle with alcoholism and the aftermath of being sexually molested just as much as they apply to my struggle with same-sex attraction. Christ is the Way to overcome any behavior or desire that can be spiritually or physically damaging, whether it is the compulsive use of food, drugs, work, or sexual activity, as well as other weaknesses and unrighteous desires. He is also the Path to freedom from the effects of abuse and other traumatic events.

Mortality brings with it circumstances that can, at times, seem impossible to overcome. We must remember who we truly are. "Satan came tempting [Moses] saying: Moses, son of man, worship me. And it came to pass that Moses looked upon Satan and said: Who art thou? For behold, I am a son of God, in the similitude of his Only Begotten." (Moses 1:12–13.)

Satan would have us believe that we are strictly the sons and daughters of man and that it is impossible to rise above genetic influences and our upbringing. Christ asks us not to accept that we are "born that way." He beckons us to follow Him and become born of God.

CHAPTER 2

MY LIFE IN A NUTSHELL

I was Mia Maid class president. I attended seminary every morning and church every Sunday. I prayed every night. I had a very strong desire to do what the Lord would have me do and to follow His example. I had a sure knowledge of the divinity of Jesus Christ, along with an undeniable testimony of the truthfulness of The Church of Jesus Christ of Latter-day Saints. And I found myself attracted to other girls.

I don't remember ever thinking, "Gee, rather than being interested in the opposite sex like everyone else and like the Lord directed, I think I'll be interested in women." It was not open rebellion. It was not a blatant attempt to disobey. I had a problem, and I didn't have the foggiest notion where it came from.

I was scared to death of my feelings and yet excited and curious about them. I discovered that my feelings were in total conflict with my beliefs. Soon I couldn't tell which were which.

Perhaps I should begin at the beginning. The first difficulties I can remember occurred when a "conflict of interest" arose between my mother and me. Neither one of us was really at fault. She would put me in fancy dresses and white patent leather shoes. I'd strip to my undies and chase polliwogs. She would buy me beautiful dolls to play with. I'd plow through the mud with my brothers' Tonka trucks. She wanted me to be a dainty little girl. I was a tomboy through and through.

Real problems began at the age of nine when an older boy in the neighborhood sexually molested me. I felt a little funny about it but went along because I liked the attention and enjoyed the touching.

The fact that I found pleasure in those experiences would come back to haunt me, serving as "proof" that I was guilty and bad.

Frustration intensified a year later when the father of a family we knew asked if I wanted to go for a ride in his car. I thought he was taking me to get ice cream. Instead, he raped me. Then he told me I had done an awful thing and should never tell anyone, not even my parents. I took his word for it. There was nothing enjoyable about that experience. It was traumatic.

Needless to say, those events had a profound effect on my life. I think I was twelve when a friend came over to tell me she'd heard sex was the worst sin, next to murder, and you could get kicked out of the Church for it.

Suddenly I realized just what that older man had meant when he said I shouldn't tell anyone about the awful thing I'd done. No wonder I shouldn't tell. I'd get kicked out of the Church—the Church that had come to mean everything to me. I couldn't understand how I could have done something so wrong when all that had ever mattered to me was choosing the right. I even had a CTR ring to prove it.

I'll never forget that day. I was sitting there, holding a stuffed kitten when my friend came over. After I heard the news, I put the kitten down and never picked up my childhood again.

The following year I received a diary for Christmas. It was my very first journal. I was excited about recording my thoughts and feelings and the events of the day. No sooner had I begun than I noticed a problem. I wanted to write about how guilty I felt—for that was the only real feeling I had—but I was afraid someone might read it. In lieu of a full confession, I decided to etch a small "g" in the upper right-hand corner of the page corresponding to the day I felt guilty. After three months, I could no longer bear to write in my diary. Every single page had a "g" in the upper right-hand corner. I threw the journal away, but day after day continued, just like the turning of pages, each bearing the mark of "guilty."

My mother gave me a book to read about the birds and the bees. I remember thinking it was a little late. When I read the part about sperm swimming to the egg to make a baby, I panicked. I was afraid that once I was old enough to make an egg, I'd get pregnant. The sperm in the photos looked like pretty tough little fish. I figured they could swim around for several years, if need be, until an egg showed up. I considered asking Mom how old sperm lived to be, but I didn't dare ask too many questions. I was afraid she might wonder why I was so curious.

I suppose I learned about the gospel in Sunday School, Mutual, and seminary classes, but the only lessons I can easily recollect are those that stressed the importance of chastity. You know the ones. If you put nails in a board, you can pull the nails back out, but there are still holes. Chew up a piece of gum, and who else in the room wants it? Which would you rather have, a new car or a used one?

The lesson I remember best was the one in which a carnation blossom was passed around the room. I was sitting in the back row and ended up with the wilted carnation everyone had man-handled. The teacher said, "See, if you break the law of chastity, you end up like that poor carnation." I wilted in my chair.

The guilt became heavier and heavier. Suicide was out of the question because that would be worse than what I'd already done. But the guilt brought on a darkness and depression that was nearly all-consuming. I say nearly all-consuming because somehow I managed to live my life as though nothing had happened. I got good grades and had lots of friends and participated in lots of activities. I could let no one suspect I was guilty of such a vile act; otherwise, I would get kicked out of the Church, humiliate my family, and lose the only things that really mattered to me.

One night I prayed as I had for a hundred nights before, begging for forgiveness. As always, I still felt guilty. Any answers Heavenly Father was sending were blocked by my certainty that to be forgiven, I had to talk with the bishop. The thought that there was nothing for which I needed to be forgiven never once crossed my mind.

When I asked Heavenly Father that night if I should go to the bishop, I heard an audible yes in reply. I suppose He knew it would take an undeniable answer to convince me.

So I "confessed." The bishop simply asked if I had known what I was doing was wrong. I told him I felt kind of funny about it at the time but that I didn't know it was such a big deal. Then he asked if the older man had "penetrated" me. I didn't know what the word meant.

That was about the extent of it. There was no recognition that I had been a ten-year-old girl who was victimized by a grown man. I received no reassurance of my innocence. I left the bishop's office relieved that I had kept my membership but horribly disappointed that I had also kept all the guilt.

During that time there was a great deal of contention at home. After years of arguing, my parents announced they would be splitting up. The next day I came home from school and noticed my dad's car and motorcycle were both gone. I walked by my parents' room and saw that the TV was missing. In a frenzy, I ran to my father's closet and flung open the doors. The closet was empty, except for a few hangers and an old pair of suspenders—the suspenders he wore on his waders when he took me fishing. I threw myself against the back of the closet and slid down to the floor. I sat there wishing I could cry, but Dad didn't believe in crying.

Our household went from one of contention to one of depression. It was an extremely difficult time for my mother. She reached out to me, and I thought she wanted my help. Unfortunately, I refused to have anything to do with her because my own ship was sinking. I figured it was every woman for herself. As my brothers and sisters went their separate ways, I came to the harsh realization that families are not always forever.

My feelings for other girls started to build as my world fell apart. Because of my testimony I refused to act on anything I felt, but it was all too much. I totally shut down, even though I went to church and went to school. I became involved in sports, which served as my escape.

Sports helped me through high school and earned me a scholarship to college. Even though by then I knew, rationally, that I wasn't responsible for the sexual abuse, guilt still formed what felt like the deepest part of me. Church seemed to offer no solutions, and whenever I was there, I felt worse about myself. Finally, I stopped attending. I couldn't take the guilt and the self-hatred anymore.

Later I found myself attracted to a girlfriend of mine, and we became involved. We never got very physical because of my

testimony, but it uncovered feelings I'd kept buried. The relationship felt so natural to me. I was not the least bit repulsed by it,
although I'd wondered if I might be. Culture and religion had
taught me well that you don't get involved with members of the
same sex: it's revolting, foul, and disgusting. I found it to be the
opposite.

The relationship didn't last long, and afterwards I turned more
and more to drugs and alcohol as alternate escape routes. I associated mostly with people living a gay lifestyle.

One day a friend introduced me to Tracy, and my whole world
changed. Finally, there was relief from the pain. I stopped hating
myself and began to feel love. I was able to express emotions after
keeping them shut down for so many years. Tracy and I were very
much alike. We related in the same ways. At church I'd felt rejection.
With Tracy I felt total acceptance. In her, I had found a refuge—
something that felt right and good in my life. At least, it felt right and
good for quite a while. Then a problem arose. My testimony of the
gospel of Jesus Christ began to surface on occasion. I tried to block it
out with Tracy or alcohol or drugs, but it kept nagging at me. I could
not become totally comfortable with the physical aspects of our relationship because of my testimony. And I was never honest with Tracy
about any of it. I kept trying to hide the conflict that was, no doubt,
quite evident.

Eventually Tracy left, I suppose in search of a more stable and
committed relationship. I became angry at God, blaming him for
causing me to go back and forth about the relationship. I decided to
embrace the lifestyle more fully.

Soon I met Kathy, and we remained involved until I moved out
of state. She flew out to see me several times. Her visits helped with
the loneliness, but between visits and drunken spells, I had a chance
to think. Christ took those moments, fleeting as they were, to work
on me. My conscience would not let me rest.

When nothing else worked, I found the ward I lived in and met
with the bishop. Soon I began meeting with Bishop Garey weekly.
He was supportive and helped me break off ties with Kathy. I started
going to church, but I didn't know anyone and felt out of place. I
was the misfit, the queer, the repulsive sinner. There I would sit,

fidgeting on the bench, hoping no one suspected who I really was and what I had done.

There's nothing lonelier than sitting in a room full of people who don't understand.

I went to Relief Society one Sunday. As the sisters filtered in, they talked and laughed with each other. I sat back and watched from behind what felt like a partition. I was the outsider looking in, observing life in Relief Society as if it were a moving diorama at a visitors center.

It was fast Sunday, and the end of class was reserved for bearing testimonies. I imagined standing up and telling them my name was Erin and I was new in the ward. I'd just started coming back to church because I was struggling with alcoholism and homosexuality. Then I imagined the whole room becoming still with that awkward, uncomfortable kind of silence that is so deafening. I imagined walking from the room when I had finished and returning to church the following week. I could hear the people laugh and see them point. I could hear them mumble under their breath and grow silent as I approached.

I squirmed in my seat.

Then I imagined being in my jeans and a sweatshirt at my old house with all my old friends, living the old lifestyle. We were talking and laughing and sharing in the latest gossip over a game of cards. I had a sense of belonging. I was around others with whom I had much in common. I actually felt good about myself, at least while I was sitting there ignoring my conscience and my testimony.

Suddenly, the Relief Society sisters started singing the closing hymn. I wiped the slight smile from my face as I realized where I was.

The Mormon Church. Would I ever belong?

By now I was drinking quite heavily. It seemed to be the only way to cope with the indescribable loneliness and darkness. I felt completely shut off from human contact and love. The bishop was a wonderful man, but he could only do so much. My pain was excruciating.

During the next six months I made some slight progress. Then Satan made a strategic move. He assisted me in believing I could handle seeing Tracy, "just to say good-bye for good." When I met with her, my feelings became stronger than ever. We decided to see each other again, and I was elated.

Even though we lived in different states, we talked on the phone every day, and she came to visit. It was incredibly wonderful to have someone in my life again. I felt whole. Relief had finally arrived. I no longer had to try to find place in a church where I felt like such a distant stranger.

About a month after I resumed my relationship with Tracy, I went to see Bishop Garey to tell him why I wasn't coming back to church. I greatly appreciated his help but had decided to remain in a homosexual relationship, "where I belonged." If he wanted to take my name off the Church records, that would suit me just fine.

After I told him, I breathed a deep sigh of relief and got up to leave. He asked if he could say something. "Sure," I said. I really did like him.

He looked angry at first. Then the Spirit took over. I got the intense feeling that the Lord was in attendance. The bishop spoke; however, the words he spoke were not his. "I say this with sincerity and with loving kindness, but I feel compelled to tell you that you're working your way straight to hell."

I was struck down. For a moment, which seemed more like an eternity, the spirit of Christ was taken from me, and I felt what real darkness and emptiness were like. The Spirit I thought had long since flickered out was still a vital life force I desperately needed.

If those words had been only the words of a bishop, I would have stormed out of the office and never looked back. I had heard more than the words of a bishop. I had received a hand-delivered message from beyond the veil. I could no longer justify or rationalize or hide behind half-truths, although I would continue to try.

To this day, I can still feel the profound effect of that message.

The darkness that fell after Bishop Garey spoke was lifted slightly when a faint glimmer of hope flickered. I sensed that Christ Himself was calling me back, begging me to come unto Him and receive His light.

Of course, there was still Tracy. And she was tough competition for a flicker of light. I could feel her love, and she was right there for me. When I prayed for comfort from heaven, I usually could not feel a thing. Tracy was tangible. The Spirit of Christ was not.

The battle that ensued was horrendous. The pain and the conflict and the darkness were intense. There was a constant struggle between what felt right and what I knew was right. I'd had a firm testimony of the gospel of Jesus Christ for as long as I could remember. I suppose it had been given to me because of the challenges I was to face. That testimony was working against me now. It had gone beyond the feeling stage and existed as a cold, hard fact. I had never doubted my testimony before. Now I had to. It lacked the "feeling" of rightness I had with Tracy. It was telling me that what felt right was actually wrong.

Refraining from seeing Tracy was more than I could handle. I cannot accurately describe the struggle, but this analogy comes close:

I was caught in a terrible storm for quite some time. Temperatures were well below freezing, and I had nothing to keep me warm. Exposed to chilling winds and blinding snow, I searched and searched for shelter but could find none. Eventually, I suffered frostbite and collapsed.

A woman found me and took me to her home. She sat with me by the fire and comforted me. We spoke of the storm, and she seemed to understand. Her company and the warmth of the fire provided the comfort and protection I had so desperately sought. I had found refuge.

After I settled in, a cold, harsh voice from outside told me I was in the wrong place and would have to go back out to find the right path. I did not trust that voice. It carried misery in its wake. I was well aware of how terrible it was out there, and this time would be worse because I knew where immediate comfort could be found.

My life became a cycle of stepping out into the cold, becoming unable to survive the storm, and running back to the only warmth and shelter I knew.

"But when he saw the wind boisterous, he was afraid; and beginning to sink, he cried, saying, Lord, save me." (Matthew 14:30.) I kept sinking.

Bishop Garey asked me if I could completely cut off my relationship with Tracy, and I said I could not. My feelings were far too strong, and I felt little comfort at church.

He asked me not to see her for a while, and that lasted for about a month. Then I felt like I couldn't handle it any longer and told the bishop I just had to see her. I assured him nothing would happen, honestly thinking nothing would. But something did happen, and I returned, confused and ashamed. He insisted that I stop seeing her, and I agreed to follow his counsel. Eventually, however, I broke down and saw her again.

This cycle continued for quite some time. I continued to abuse alcohol in an attempt to fix the pain and build a bridge across the great abyss. The pain was debilitating. The darkness was all-consuming. It was as if my very identity was being ripped apart. I suppose that's exactly what happened.

When I needed strength from the Lord, I often could not grasp it. I believe He was holding out His hand, but I felt terribly unworthy to respond. I mistakenly believed His love had to be earned.

The heavens were as brass. The conflict had no end. I endured months of agonizing turmoil. What felt right was wrong. What felt wrong was right. Nothing made any sense, and nobody had any real answers. No one could help.

In desperation, I took the gun I used for protection from beneath my bed. I pulled back the hammer and placed the tip of the barrel at the back of my mouth. I rested my finger on the trigger. My entire life did not pass before my eyes, just the agony of the moment and the recent past. I could think of happy times, reasons to live, but they were all from a lifetime now forbidden. I figured that if I was going to hell, I should just get it over with.

Try as I might, I could not pull the trigger. It was neither cowardice nor bravery that stopped me. It was an impression that came into my mind—the impression that a bullet would not stop the turmoil. I needed to fight the battle on this frontier.

With that impression came a little ammunition—hope. From somewhere came the reassurance that life would not always be so horrific. And it wasn't. The anguish would subside for a time and then come back with a vengeance. When things became unbearable,

I would take out the gun. Each attempt to pull the trigger was unsuccessful.

I remember lying in bed, unable even to sit up and write in my journal. I used journal writing as a release on occasion, no longer worried about who might read it. Many pages consisted of chicken scribbles slanting down the page.

Pain seldom stays within the lines.

I'd grown weary of trying to leave Tracy when I couldn't feel any love from Christ. There were many, many dark and empty days. I questioned whether I could make it and felt I was fighting the inevitable. "I am gay," I would cry, in an attempt to get God to face facts.

> Dear God, it's black again.
> Two solid months of darkness.
> Two solid days of light marked Christ's arrival.
>
> I guess He isn't coming.
>
> Have faith, you say?
> But faith does not hold my hand.
> Or stroke my hair and tell me I'm OK.
>
> God, if this is wrong,
> Then where's thy love when heaven's touch
> Feels cold as brass?
>
> And if this flame that lights my heart
> Is Satan's fire, I cannot tell.
> Sheep's clothing warms my soul.
>
> You say to change.
> I say I can't.
> I feel, therefore I am.

The most intense part of the struggle lasted for more than two years. Many, many times I felt I could not go on.

I used to sit in my tiny room, which had a solitary chair with my scriptures next to it. When I felt as if I was going to die—which could occur several times in a day—I would go into that room and

read. Somehow, some way, the scriptures helped. They were an I.V.
drip, providing just enough nutrients to keep me alive.

Drip.

Drip.

Drip.

I wanted to "feast upon the words of Christ," but I was not
accustomed to finding nourishment the Lord's way. So it came, drip
by drip, line upon line, here a little, there a little. It never seemed to
be enough. I was always in pain. But I kept going back to the scriptures for more nourishment because I was finally acting on faith.

My bishop was another source of strength and light. I sat on the
front steps of the chapel every Wednesday night, waiting for him to
arrive. I usually signed up for the earliest appointment so I could be
the first to see him. He'd walk up and give me a nourishing embrace.
Then he'd unlock the door and escort me into the church. It was
dark, and he'd turn on the light. I remember thinking how
symbolic that was. My life was dark except for when the bishop
turned on the light.

He'd ask me how I was doing. He'd smile and say something
encouraging. Even when I'd fallen, he would offer support. As the
Spirit emanated from him, I basked in the light. I loved those
twenty minutes with him and hated to have them end.

My prayers started to break through the cloud cover on occasion, too. I would humbly kneel in prayer many times a day, begging
for strength. Heavenly Father was the One person with whom I
could be completely honest. My anger toward Him started to diminish as I befriended Him and felt His continual attempts to befriend
me.

I finally found the nerve to open up to a friend of mine from
Church. I told her I'd struggled with homosexual desires and alcoholism. She was supportive and discreet. Her reaction encouraged
me to tell another friend. It was such a welcome relief to spend time
with two Mormon women who knew all about me and accepted me
anyway. I began to feel a sense of belonging in a church that had
once felt so rejecting.

Finding people who were Christlike in their responses helped
me better understand how the gospel was designed to work in my

life. I learned not to lump everything into the term "the Church." I realized that the gospel was something different from the people at church, including some leaders, who misunderstood the issue of same-sex attraction.

The first part of the battle was pitch black. Then glimmers of light came from prayer, the scriptures, helping others, being helped by others, and meeting with the bishop. As I did those things sporadically, light came in brief flashes—each adding to the next. Unfortunately, the effects were slight, and I could not see at the time that change was taking place.

Just when I thought I was doing better, a bad day or week or month would come along and slam me up against the wall. I'd start questioning everything again. Was I really improving? Would I always be miserable? Was all this effort doing any good? Then I'd decide prayer and scripture reading weren't helping, and I'd stop completely for months on end.

There were no life-altering events, only waves of dark and light, weakness and strength, that passed through my life at varying frequencies. It was a gradual uphill climb filled with peaks and valleys.

The peaks slowly, imperceptibly, began to outnumber the valleys, even those valleys of the shadow of death, where suicide pounded at my door. Improvement was slow and unsteady. My patience and faith were being tried.

If I were to graph my progress over those years (throwing all scientific accuracy to the wind), it would look something like this:

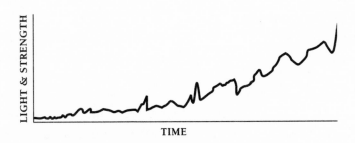

That's how it appears with hindsight. Back then, whenever I was down, it seemed I was as low as I'd been the time before and therefore was making no progress. Year after year, as the good days became slightly more frequent, the bad days became more obvious. They often seemed as low as ever because I had the good days with which to compare them. In reality, my lowest lows became less and less deep.

With determined effort and power from heaven, my visits with Tracy became less frequent. It was a blessing that we lived in different states.

After about a year and a half of trying to end the relationship, I discovered that although the sexual involvement had recently stopped, I was still affected by my feelings for her. I recorded in my journal, "I shouldn't have gone to see her. It's like going through a time warp. So much for controlling my thoughts. I am at the mercy of my old self. Since seeing her I've lost the independence and self-assuredness I had gained. I've lost the old one-two punch. Any progress I make seems to be erased whenever I cross the border. I need to let go of the past and move on to my present.

"My attitudes have been fluctuating with the wind. Decision, no decision—out of control. Fortunately, today things seem to be calming down. I watched some of general conference, and I know that helped a lot. I haven't been adding to my spiritual file as I should. Whenever I slack off, the rest of my life suffers."

The less I saw of Tracy, the more I leaned on alcohol, tobacco, and marijuana. But I was finally able to stop seeing her. We continued talking on the phone, however. I still loved her—often as a dear friend—for she was a very good person. Yet try as I might, I could not let go of the more intense feelings I had for her. I desperately needed something or someone to lean on, and the Lord's way was taking too long.

When I stopped seeing Tracy, I replaced her with a serious addiction to alcohol. Soon I couldn't last longer than a week without getting drunk. I sincerely tried to stop, but I was unable to bear the anguish and intense loneliness that continually returned to haunt me.

Once I managed to go for thirty-nine days without a drink. Thirty-nine whole days. It was a record. When I told the bishop, he expressed sincere congratulations, and I felt proud—for a few minutes. Then Satan started working on me. All the way home I kept thinking, "Thirty-nine days, and it's driven you crazy! You've been climbing the walls and praying all the time and reading scriptures and you've only gone thirty-nine days. You need to go an eternity without alcohol, and thirty-nine days already seems like an eternity!" I stopped at the liquor store on my way home.

Often when I started making real progress, I'd do something that set me back. I went on vacation to visit some of my college friends in the city where Tracy lived. She was out of town for the weekend but would return on Monday. I wasn't scheduled to go back home until Tuesday, so I figured I'd see her. By Sunday I felt that seeing her wasn't such a good idea. We hadn't been physically involved for many months, but I felt I should leave town before she arrived. What? Couldn't I handle it? Was I still gay? Was I never going to be happy without her? Would the struggle never end?

There seemed to be more questions than answers, so I sought the opinion of six of my closest friends—a six-pack of beer. I hopped into my car and began to drive to the next state. Somewhere along the way I finished the six-pack and got another. Somewhere else along the way I went off the road and totaled my car. A paramedic had to pull me out, but I walked away without a scratch.

You've heard the news stories. Some drunken idiot slams into a sedan with a mother and kids. Everyone in the sedan is killed, but the lush, because he was drunk and relaxed, walks off without a scratch. Gratefully, mine was a one-car accident. Still, I couldn't help but think about what I'd narrowly missed and who I was—a drunkard who gives no thought for human life. I added that to my list of damaging labels.

The wreck cured me of my drinking—for about a week and a half. I'd quit praying and reading the scriptures and was continuing to search for ways to feel better about myself immediately. Satan was happy to step in again. I met Brent, and we became good friends. He abused cocaine and wanted someone to party with on occasion. I wasn't about to pass up free cocaine.

The worst part about cocaine was that it made me feel better about myself, at least while I was high. Under its influence I felt as though I could succeed at life, a condition that contrasted sharply with my usual feelings of failure. Once again, I quickly grew accustomed to seizing the opportunity for a "quick fix" rather than working through the long, painful process of repentance.

One evening Brent and I finished off the cocaine by about 2:30 in the morning. I wasn't ready to quit feeling good about myself as I came down from the "high," so when Brent offered to take me to his supplier's house, I readily agreed. We took a cab to the heart of a drug neighborhood. I was nervous, but my need to feel good was greater than my fear. Brent told the cabby to pull over. The driver asked, "Miss, are you sure you want to get out here? This is a dangerous neighborhood." Oh yes, I wanted to get out there, thank you.

We went in, met the dealer, and Brent asked for rock cocaine—the form in which it is smoked. I'd never smoked cocaine before, but I knew it was dangerous. I don't remember exactly how it was done, only that at some point it involved rinsing something with alcohol and then lighting it, which would create a rather sudden "flash" of fire. Nearly all the house lights were out to avoid suspicion because the area was frequently patrolled. The woman's grandfather sat in a rocker, peeking through a slit in the curtains to watch for cops. He would alert us if a car drove by, so we'd know not to light up or create a "flash."

We smoked cocaine all through the rest of the night. The sun came up, and a little later the woman's young son walked into the room. I was aghast that he came in while we were doing drugs. He said to his mom, "Do you want me to make another run?" "Yes, hurry," was the reply. Brent handed him a fistful of hundred dollar bills, and he skipped off as if he were going over to the neighbor's to borrow a couple of eggs or something.

He was eight or nine, around baptismal age. Seeing him was the final straw. I watched that kid run out the door, and I looked at that grandpa peering through the curtains, and as the light made its way through the slit in those curtains, I felt the strongest desire to be home. I'm not sure whose home I had in mind. I just wanted to be in a good Mormon home where the kids went off to Primary to learn about the Savior and grandpa sat in an easy chair reading the latest *Ensign*.

Now the situations were reversed. Instead of sitting in church wishing I could be partying with all my friends, I was partying with all my friends wishing I could be at church. The desire was fleeting, but it cured me of my cocaine habit.

I still continued to drink, though. I'd love to say an experience like the car wreck or the trip to the drug neighborhood totally changed my life. I kept hoping for the big miracle, but while I was looking for it, I missed the smaller ones. I was not attuned to subtle messages from the Spirit. What I wanted was a real miracle: Take away all my pain and my sinful desires, tonight!

As another year passed, the good days became more frequent. I began to feel more strength from within and from the Lord, as I started praying and reading the scriptures again. I also felt more opposition. By now I was writing in my journal such things as "Life has been so intense lately. I was asked to give a Relief Society lesson on joy a couple of weeks ago. I stayed up the whole night before. It was amazing. For the first time in my life I enjoyed the time with the Lord more than other things. That's a breakthrough. As low as my life has been lately, those lows have been buffered by feelings in the opposite direction. At least things are extreme in both directions now, rather than just downward. Perhaps I have to be continually reminded of my dependence on the Lord. Whatever the reasons, I know everything really has been laid out by Him. And maybe I don't get to set things exactly how I want them, but the One who did can choose better than I."

About this time I received a job offer in another state. I hated to leave Bishop Garey and my friends after three and a half years of their support. I'd stopped seeing Tracy. I'd stopped going to places where I was more likely to meet women seeking homosexual relationships, and I'd consciously and consistently worked on not thinking of other women in ways I shouldn't.

Bishop Garey felt inspired that I should take the job, so I packed my belongings and moved to a new city, determined to start a new life. I sat again as a stranger in another ward with another bishop. I prayed and read the scriptures occasionally, but I became very lonely.

I returned to my old "friends," alcohol and marijuana, although I did find a few casual, human friends. Bishop Garey remained my greatest support via telephone.

Two months after the move I wrote: "I have lost so much time. Can I ever regain it? Will I ever become the person the Lord and I want me to be? It seems like I have so far to go. Perhaps it always seems to be that way. Once again, the key word is patience. I'm just sick and tired of being patient."

After several more months in the new city, I managed to turn completely to the Lord and stop drinking. I'd gone several weeks without a drink and considered calling my former bishop to tell him. I knew he'd be very pleased, but I decided to wait till I'd gone even longer. Then a friend in my old ward called to tell me that Bishop Garey had died in a tragic accident.

I went numb.

I was unable to respond.
Or think.
Or, put

one

word where it belonged
after another word
or before.   Should it be before?

Why? Why me? Why him? WHY? WHY? WHY?

I flew in for the funeral. I didn't cry until I sat on the church steps and found myself thinking that if I just sat there and waited long enough, surely the bishop would pull up and come over to give me a nourishing embrace and walk me into the dark chapel and turn on the light for me and say I was going to make it through and I'd believe him. I could always believe him. He was always there when I needed him.

After the funeral, they carried his coffin out of the chapel and turned off my light. Hope disappeared into the bleakness. My faith was buried along with my bishop.

The battle became horrifying again. The darkness was unbearable. Once again I stopped praying and reading the scriptures. I felt emptier and emptier as I poured more and more alcohol into the void. I managed to work all day, and then I'd drink all night. Suicide became an option again. I'd show God He had pushed me too far this time. I'd really show Him. How could He take Bishop Garey away just when I was making progress? I'd learned to find support and comfort through "appropriate relationships" and look where that had gotten me. I'd made many sacrifices. God owed me. He had no right to be taking more things away. I'd tried my hardest for nearly four years, and I was left with more darkness and misery. Why should I keep trying it God's way? I hadn't seen any mighty changes, only mighty pain. How could any of it be true?

About three months after Bishop Garey died, Heavenly Father lovingly stepped in again—the same Heavenly Father I had refused to trust, the One I was so angry with I'd stopped talking to, the One whose church I'd quit attending. His Holy Spirit broke through the anger and inspired me to call a counselor.

Once again someone was brought into my life just in time to help. Many of my feelings for Tracy and other women had surfaced again. I didn't act on them because I was feeling suicidal. I feared that a homosexual relationship would add to my distress, which, in turn, could easily put me over the edge. I seriously doubted I could continue to avoid homosexual relationships. I doubted I could ever overcome alcoholism. I doubted I could do the "church bit" again.

Miraculously, Pam—my counselor—started to bring hope back into my life. She had a very strong spirit, and I could feel it. As with Bishop Garey, I gained strength from sitting in a room with someone who was exercising the gifts of the Holy Spirit in my behalf. I couldn't go on borrowed light forever, but unable as I was to feel light from within, it helped to feel it from without.

Pam also offered practical counsel that helped with my alcohol abuse and homosexual feelings. I quit taking a Pollyanna view of homosexual relationships and thought of the turmoil they caused instead of just the comfort they provided. I made the effort to stop considering those relationships as options. I concentrated on what I truly wanted out of life, and Pam helped me believe I could attain it. I looked at myself more positively, and the self-hatred began to subside. I attended Alcoholics Anonymous. I read the scriptures again. I prayed again. I went back to church and served wherever I could. Gradually, line upon line—once again—light entered my life. I became stronger and stronger as my desires to drink and to return to a homosexual life got weaker and weaker.

After I had gone about a month without drinking, I talked to Pam about how much I missed Bishop Garey. I said I wished he was around to offer advice. She suggested that I write a letter as if it were from him. The veil was thin that day, and the words of the bishop came into my mind. I felt his presence and recorded eight pages of his inspiration and support. I seemed to hear a promise that I would never again become trapped by alcoholism or homosexual relationships.

The following week I was laid off work. My first reaction was to stop at the liquor store on my way home, but there were those promises from Bishop Garey.

I managed to remain sober for the two months I was unemployed. It took every ounce of strength I could muster. I prayed constantly. I was more determined and more able than ever. Those two months left me feeling that if I could survive unemployment without a woman in my life and without alcohol, I could survive anything. For the first time, I gained confidence in my ability to overcome.

I spent the following year and a half, sober and free from homosexual relationships. It was a long year and a half. There were times when each second of each minute of each hour of each day of each week ticked slowly and loudly by. Whenever I was tempted, I'd think of how much I hated myself after I succumbed. I went on pure faith. I continued to pray and read scriptures, even when I thought they were not helping. I kept believing that life would eventually get easier, once enough seconds and minutes and hours and days and weeks had gone by. Even though I thought I could not bear it, in time I found I could.

I was now talking to Tracy on the phone every other month or so. I spent very little time thinking about her and seldom thought of other women. It required conscious effort, which often proved to be exhausting. I concentrated on other things. I read the scriptures. I became very involved in my work—too much so at times. When I couldn't handle life, I would work ridiculously long hours. I had not dealt with much of the anger or pain or guilt that had built up for so many years. I was still seeing Pam, but we dealt mostly with my efforts to remain sober and chaste.

After a year and a half of sobriety I wrote: "Flashes of normalcy are becoming more frequent and staying longer. I haven't been happier than this since I was nine years old. Work is going lousy, but there is inner peace. It's like the blanket of heavy snow that smothered my soul is thawing, loosening its death grip. Life is springing forth from a seed that was buried deep, before the winter storm hit. The warmth of the gentle Son beckons me on and reassures me. It's all so new. Life has been breathed into me again."

I remained sober until I went on vacation with a friend who, unbeknownst to me, brought along marijuana. We were far away from home, and I didn't have my own car. He didn't quite understand why it was such a big deal that I refrain from smoking pot. I lasted about a day and a half before I gave in and went on a three-week binge.

That I had succumbed to substance abuse after abstaining for so long hit me very hard. I felt like a failure again. Then I made a commitment to refrain from drugs and alcohol for another year. I decided that after the year was up, I could take a "week off" to drink and do drugs. Looking back, I can see that was a poor decision, but at the time, I didn't want to suffer the tremendous blow of another failure. I guess I thought if I planned to succumb after a year, it wouldn't really be a failure. I had confidence I could last a year because I'd already made it a year and a half.

My confidence served as a foundation after the three-week binge. Not all of my progress had been destroyed. Church attendance and prayer and time spent sober with supportive friends had strengthened me.

Three months after the binge I recorded: "There is a stream of unconsciousness that flows deep within me. It's the love of God and my faith in that power. When things get really tough, I can bend down and sip from those waters, gaining a renewed strength. I'm helped by a comparison to life a few years back, which seems like an eternity ago. Then the well was dry—nothing but a black, awful pit that seemed to swallow me up and leave me with nowhere to go. I thank God I now have somewhere to go."

The nine months of sobriety that followed were amazing. I started treating myself kindly for the first time. I began to discover who I was. I attended my new ward whenever I was in town and accepted a calling. I read my scriptures and prayed. I served others somewhat but spent greatly needed time serving myself. I even felt I deserved it.

Most of the surface pain had subsided, and I spent my weekends doing whatever I wanted to, as long as it was within the Lord's boundaries. Previously, my only sources of "happiness" were outside those boundaries, so I had some relearning to do. I felt like a little kid as I visited national parks and reserves and zoos and museums and mountains and beaches. It was, quite literally, a whole new world for me.

As the year mark approached, I began to be filled with angst. I struggled again not to drink because I knew I'd be drinking for a week when the year was up and I couldn't seem to change my plan. It carried with it a downward force that gained more and more momentum as the time approached.

I feared the binge might not be confined to one week. I knew if it weren't, emotional upheaval and destruction would follow. I fervently prayed for strength. The previous year had brought me a grander, eternal perspective that caused me to look back on my past life with fear and trembling, not with fond remembrances.

My deadline arrived. I took a week's "vacation" with a friend, and we drank and smoked pot much of the time. Parts of it were enjoyable, but there was an underlying fear. When the week was up I wrote: "I called Pam a few weeks ago. I told her how I'd gone a year free from substance abuse but that I'd be partying again for a week. She told me to make sure I planned a celebration for the next year, something exceptional that didn't include any foreign substances. I'm going to go through the temple next year and then take a temple trip to Hawaii or Canada to celebrate. I've decided to commit, and I have never regretted a decision to do the right thing. God, I need your help with all this."

I made the commitment to Heavenly Father that I would stop drinking and smoking and doing drugs and being involved with women forever. I don't know how many times I had said that prayer—honestly wanting to commit and stick to it but never finding the strength. This time the previous years of my mostly righteous living served me well. The screaming voice was finally silenced—the voice that insisted, "You'll never be able to do what you've promised, you fool! You'll never give all of this up. You'll fail again, just like you always do."

I had traveled a difficult road to make such progress. I knew how horrible slipping up or trying to change direction made me feel. And, most importantly, I'd begun to be fed by the Spirit as I gradually learned to meet my needs in righteous ways.

The Savior's atonement began to bear full sway in my heart. I wanted a life with Christ. I did not want the alternative. And now I could see clearly enough to know I had to make a choice.

The repentance that followed carried a greater power to transform me than I had ever known. My desire to attend the temple soared, so I met with my bishop to discuss the possibility. After a number of meetings and a sufficient period of time, he determined I was worthy to attend the temple. I received my endowments almost three years ago, and I've kept those covenants ever since.

Once I had gone through the temple, I attended every week. Overall, life was good. Yet, occasionally I still longed for the things that had brought comfort or had been a means of escape in the past. I was tempted most often when I felt stressed or tired, so I learned to take great care to avoid both.

When I attended the temple, I drew unto the Spirit as never before. My goal had been to sacrifice homosexual relationships and alcohol completely before I died. I'd decided that was my life's mission.

That was just the beginning.

Attending the temple made me aware of more and more things I needed to sacrifice. I gave up a well-paying job to find one that would give me more time to come unto Christ. I stopped seeing R-rated movies. I devoted more and more of my energy and talents to the Church. And just when I'd reached a point where I could be perfectly happy spending my time on a mountaintop watching the breeze go by, I was asked to sacrifice most of my free time. But sacrifice after sacrifice brought forth blessing after blessing.

The temple held great cleansing power—not just cleansing from sin but cleansing from pain and anger and all the rest of it. The light and knowledge I received in the temple uncovered the darkness I still held within. I found emotions and weaknesses I needed to work through. I was surprised to discover I had to go back to feelings and events I thought I'd already overcome. Because of the power of the temple and righteous living, I gained greater insight and strength, which enabled me to recognize and deal with feelings at a deeper level. The process was important because I was able to release what held me bound to sinful desires. There were times while I was unleashing those feelings that sinful desires became stronger than they had been in years. They were still attached at a deeper level. It took determination, sheer willpower, and divine assistance to ride out the days, weeks, and even months when my feelings and desires were exposed with great intensity. I needed all the strength I had gathered, and I'm certain I could not have withstood the force of those temptations any earlier in my life.

I also discovered there was intense anger and guilt left over from the abuse and the same-sex attraction. I had not completely forgiven myself, Heavenly Father, and others for certain circumstances and events. So, with the help of a friend and a counselor, I uprooted, worked through, and cast off the junk I had left inside. I wanted to be pure, and I was willing to go through the pain and effort required.

As I have done all I can to remove unrighteous desires and whatever they were attached to, those desires have been removed. I now obey the law of sacrifice, the law of chastity, and the Word of Wisdom with very little resistance from within. They come "naturally" to me. I do not entertain old thoughts at all because I know where they lead, and I do not wish to follow them there.

I used to think that someday I'd discover the big secret to overcoming same-sex attraction and alcoholism. After I had searched high and low for the miracle cure, I finally learned the cure comes step by step, each small gain a miracle in itself. "And thus we see that by small means the Lord can bring about great things." (1 Nephi 16:29.)

Change occurred gradually and nearly imperceptibly. The darkness was abated slowly as the light increased ever so slightly. The longer I stayed away from inappropriate relationships with women, the easier it became to live without them. The more time I spent with the Spirit instead of drinking or doing drugs, the stronger I became.

My quest for the miracle cure and the answers to the grand mysteries of life brought me back to the things I'd learned in Primary. I discovered that miracles occur and knowledge is revealed when we consistently obey plain and simple truths: Prayer, scripture study, church attendance, and counseling with those guided by the Spirit. Faith, hope, and charity. Repentance and obedience. Patience and endurance.

Eternal truth is one eternal round.

There were no big secrets, no grand events—as measured by earthly means. It was a long, arduous process of doing fewer of the things I wasn't supposed to do and more of the things I was, ceasing to consider the alternatives as alternatives and working with a counselor to uproot and deal with the struggles buried within. I had to give my all and more. But it was Jesus Christ who marvelously and miraculously transformed my life in ways I could not. He is my Rock and my Salvation.

The process is extremely difficult and can take years. There is no quick and easy way through it, but there is a way. Jesus Christ promises us: "I am the way, the truth, and the life." (John 14:6.)

Those who seek freedom from same-sex attraction can experience the mighty change and enjoy the great calm it brings if they are willing to put forth the effort. And to those who aren't sure it's worth the effort, I bear witness that it is.

CHAPTER 3

"Am I Gay?"

I can't count how many times I asked myself, "Am I gay?" Whenever I considered life from a spiritual perspective, I felt guilty and despised. I thought I probably was "gay," and "the Church" didn't accept me. The more rejection I perceived, the more isolation I felt.

My bishop's acceptance of me was a turning point. I learned that although he and Jesus Christ despise the sin, they love the sinner. I began to accept myself despite my homosexual attractions. I separated my identity from the sins I had committed.

Satan would have us identify with sin. Christ would have us turn away from sin and identify with Him.

Perhaps the single most important thing I realized was this: The conflict is not a matter of a "homosexual" struggling with feelings of spirituality; rather, it's the spiritual self struggling with feelings of homosexuality.

THE "GAY IDENTITY"

To avoid the conflict between same-sex attraction and a testimony of the gospel of Jesus Christ, some Church members resign themselves to the "fact" that they're "gay." It's understandable, given the direction much of the world is taking and the great pain and effort required to put off the natural self when that involves strong, binding, homosexual attractions.

The following is an oversimplification, but it illustrates how the "gay identity" sometimes develops within Mormons who struggle with same-sex attraction. It is based on my own experience and that of others I have talked with.

As youngsters, some start to feel "different" from other kids, having dissimilar interests or feelings of not fitting in. They notice attractions toward members of the same sex. Once hormones start raging, they find it difficult to figure out the reasons for their homosexual feelings, if they even label them as such.

Feelings intensify, and some individuals start acting out sexually. They believe in the gospel, yet they're told that what they're feeling is wrong. "How can feelings be wrong? They just are."

There doesn't seem to be anyone in the Church in whom they can confide. Confusion, guilt, rejection, and increased feelings of being different set in. They know The Church of Jesus Christ of Latter-day Saints disapproves, but their homosexual desires are the strongest, most convincing feelings they have.

As the years go by, they may continue to act on those feelings or at least remain very aware of them. They seek a place to belong. If it is difficult to fit in with a group of heterosexuals, it becomes even more difficult to fit in with a group of Mormon heterosexuals, a group that openly denounces homosexuality. Love and acceptance— a sense of belonging—are basic human needs. But for members of The Church of Jesus Christ of Latter-day Saints, it is difficult to feel love and acceptance and have homosexual feelings at the same time.

Something must happen. The obvious solution is to get rid of the same-sex desires. So the individuals leave homosexual relationships or try to ignore their homosexual desires and start going to church. There, they feel they're putting on a plastic Mormon facade. They are strangers there, feeling horribly empty and unfulfilled. Attempts to suppress their feelings bring only misery. It seems as though God never comes through. He doesn't do His part. "Where is the peace and the joy? Where is the mighty change? Where are the miracles?"

Disillusioned, they return to where they feel they belong—in a homosexual relationship. The search for a true identity is well underway, if that identity is not already established.

The more they think about or act on their homosexual desires, the more convinced they become that they are "homosexual."

To help set I AM GAY or I'M A LESBIAN even deeper in stone, they find that once they fully embrace this "fact," their whole world falls into place. They no longer feel different. Instead of hating themselves for having homosexual feelings, they love themselves—possibly for the first time in their lives. Instead of being ashamed, they're proud. They tell straight friends and family members. Some, exhilarated by this process, join pro-gay groups and defend their new cause. In an effort to heal old wounds, they demand the acceptance they never felt while growing up. "Healing" comes as a welcome relief. It even seems spiritual because healing is a spiritual process.

Their open declaration can feel so exhilarating, so liberating, so confirming, and so full of acceptance when there has been none, that to suggest it is false can seem preposterous to many. Satan manages to convince them: "No need to worry. The Church will come to accept homosexual relationships, and if it doesn't, it's not the true church anyway. Yes, you are gay. At long last, the truth has made you free." They believe they have found freedom by coming out of the dark closet of secrets and lies and stepping into what seems to be the light.

In actuality, it is artificial light. And it is not spiritual freedom but another huge link that has been forged in the chain that binds them to a homosexual life.

Our thoughts and behavior help form our identity. The "action which defines a man, describes his character, is action which has been repeated over and over and so has come in time to be a coherent and relatively independent mode of behavior. . . .

"Such a mode of action tends to maintain itself, to resist change. A thief is one who steals; stealing extends and reinforces the identity of thief, which generates further thefts, which further strengthen and deepen the identity. So long as one lives, change is possible; but the longer such behavior is continued the more force and authority it acquires." What applies here to stealing also applies to many other ways of thinking and behaving that result in an assumed identity.

"The identity defined by action is present and past; it may also foretell the future, but not necessarily." After we gain "the sense of an identity that has existed all along, and in some sense we knew it but would not let ourselves know that we knew it," we suddenly come to the conclusion that "'I really am a crook!' or 'I really am a coward!' We may then go too far and conclude that this identity is our 'nature,' that it was writ in the stars or in the double helix, that it transcends experience, that our actual lives have been the fulfilling of a preexisting pattern.

"In fact it was writ only in our past choices. We are wise to believe it difficult to change, to recognize that character has a forward propulsion which tends to carry it unaltered into the future, but we need not believe it impossible to change. . . .

"When we admit that those 'gifts' were bribes and say, 'Well, then, I'm a crook,' we have stated a fact, not a destiny; if we then invoke the leopard that can't change his spots, saying; 'That's just the way I am, might as well accept it,' we abandon the freedom to change and exploit what we have been in the past to avoid responsibility for what we shall be in the future.

"Often we do not choose, but drift into those modes which eventually define us. Circumstances push and we yield." (Allen Wheelis, *How People Change* [New York: Harper & Row, 1973], pp. 11–14.)

NOT BY CHOICE

Some people, inside and outside the Church, are under the common misperception that a person consciously chooses to have homosexual feelings. My experience is that, in most cases, this is simply not the case. Yet this view has created feelings of alienation among Church members struggling with same-sex attraction.

Why would someone who has a strong conviction of the divine origins of The Church of Jesus Christ of Latter-day Saints choose to engage in a wrenching conflict with that testimony, a conflict so great that often they see suicide as the only solution? Same-sex desires create a very difficult challenge for Church members and are seldom chosen. The trial befalls even the valiant ones. I have been deeply impressed by the spirituality of Church members I have met who struggle with this issue yet who find themselves trying to overcome an extremely difficult challenge.

In some cases a person does choose to develop and foster homosexual desires, but that is the exception, not the rule. An example of

this is found among women—including a few women's rights
activists—who choose to form a lesbian relationship to make themselves completely independent from men.

Most people who are attracted to the same sex will agree that
they never made a conscious choice to feel that way, just as most
heterosexually oriented people cannot remember making a conscious decision to be attracted to the opposite sex. Same-sex attraction is rarely a matter of choice. Seeking freedom from compelling
homosexual desires and behavior is a choice that can be made, but
that is no simple matter.

BORN THAT WAY?

Many insist homosexual feelings and behaviors are "natural."
That may be precisely the right word for it. "For the natural man is
an enemy to God, and has been from the fall of Adam, and will be,
forever and ever, unless he yields to the enticings of the Holy Spirit,
and putteth off the natural man . . . and becometh as a child, submissive, meek, humble, patient, full of love." (Mosiah 3:19.)

People who struggle with homosexual desires aren't the only
ones asked to overcome inborn tendencies to sin. We are all born
with a natural self whose inclination is to sin. Genetic and environmental factors create predispositions toward a variety of sins.
Different people confront different factors; hence, we each struggle
with our own unique set of challenges.

Several scientific studies have sought to find a genetic or biological link to homosexual orientation. Other studies have attempted to
link, or have actually linked, a variety of traits or behaviors to a variety of biological and genetic factors.

Many genetic factors contribute to who we are and how we feel,
whether the result is sin or positive behavior. Heavenly Father asks
us to overcome the sinful desires and foster the desires to do good,
no matter how much our natural self fights back.

We are morally obliged to conform our behavior to certain
guidelines—even when genetics are factored in. For instance, sound
scientific evidence shows that some people are genetically predis-
posed toward alcoholism—born with those tendencies. Genetics
has made the charge to obey the Word of Wisdom a more difficult

one for them, yet they are still asked to obey. (It's interesting to note that the most successful program ever developed for overcoming alcoholism is Alcoholics Anonymous, whose members claim total dependence on a "higher power" to help them return to wholeness.)

Research concerning the causes of same-sex attraction is not yet conclusive. Contributing factors may begin after conception, at birth, during early childhood, during adolescence, or later. Nevertheless, that does not mean homosexual desires are a premortal or a permanent condition or that God approves of acting on them.

In reference to our test of mortality, Elder Bruce R. McConkie states that "we would be subject to the ills of the flesh, and *there would be passions, appetites, and desires planted in the mortal body that were not there when we were in the preexistent sphere*. . . . Back there we walked by sight. Down here we walk by faith, and we have to believe and obey the Holy Gospel when it's taught to us by the Lord's representatives. We no longer have the personal knowledge that the truths are coming from God. Back there we were tried and examined and on probation as spirit beings. Down here we're on probation as mortals, where appetites control our bodies, where we have lusts, and where we're subject to hunger, thirst, fatigue, disease, sexual appetites, and all the rest." (Address delivered at the University of Utah, Salt Lake City, 10 Jan. 1982; emphasis added.)

Satan uses the message the media sends out—"homosexuals are born that way"—to promote the "logical" conclusions that "God has made them that way" and changing their sexual orientation would "go against nature." We must be careful not to let the media, or Satan, or anyone else distract us from eternal principles and cause us to ignore or rationalize what Heavenly Father has already revealed.

The natural self is a condition of mortality. Our test here on earth is to put off the carnal, natural self and become "as a child," born of God. Heavenly Father has not cheated anyone out of the opportunity to overcome sin and live a fulfilling life within the boundaries He has set. For those "born of God, [are] changed from their carnal and fallen state, to a state of righteousness, being redeemed of God, becoming his sons and daughters." (Mosiah 27: 25.)

CONTRIBUTING FACTORS

Psychologists, sociologists, biologists, geneticists, lawyers, politicians, and religious leaders all have differing opinions about the causes of same-sex attraction. There is, however, one point of agreement—there is no single cause. Same-sex attraction is the result of a variety of contributing factors, including biological, psychological, and/or environmental factors. Although generalizations always fall short, and much is still not known, the following is a brief discussion of some of the factors that may contribute to same-sex attraction.

Biological and genetic factors

Let me first state that none of the scientific findings have conclusively proven that biology or genetics contribute to homosexual inclinations. But even if conclusive scientific evidence is brought forward to show homosexual tendencies are biologically or genetically determined, it won't change a thing, except to make it easier for Satan to convince people that gaining freedom from same-sex attraction is impossible.

In 1991, Simon LeVay of the Salk Institute researched the region of the brain that is believed to regulate male sexual behavior. He examined nineteen homosexually oriented men who had died of AIDS. He found that this region of their brains averaged about half the size of the region in heterosexually oriented males and that the region was about the same size as that in women. There is no way to determine whether that difference caused the homosexual orientation or was a result of it, and AIDS could have affected the results. No definite conclusions can be drawn. ("A Difference in Hypothalamic Structure between Heterosexual and Homosexual Man," *Science* 253 [1991]: 1034–37.)

Even though it is possible that there are structural differences in the brains of some people struggling with same-sex attraction, it is also possible that those differences need not be permanent. Kenneth Klivington, also of the Salk Institute, states that "the brain's neural networks reconfigure themselves in response to certain experiences. One fascinating NIH [National Institutes of Health] study found that in people reading Braille after becoming blind, the area of the brain controlling the reading finger grew larger. . . .

"From the study of animals, we know that circulating sex hormones in the mother can have a profound effect on the organization of the brain of the fetus. Once the individual is born, the story gets more complex because of the interplay between the brain and experience. It's a feedback loop; the brain influences behavior, behavior shapes experience, experience affects the organization of the brain, and so forth." ("Born or Bred?" *Newsweek,* 24 Feb. 1992, p. 50.)

A study of homosexually oriented twin brothers found that if one identical twin was oriented toward homosexual behavior, the chances were nearly three times greater that the other twin was also, compared to the rate of fraternal twins both being homosexually oriented. Although the ratios indicate there may be a genetic link, in half the cases the identical twin brothers of homosexually oriented men were heterosexually oriented. This evidence suggests that genetics could very well play a role in sexual orientation, but it also indicates that genetics alone is not the sole determinant. (J. M. Bailey and R. C. Pillard, "A Genetic Study of Male Sexual Orientation," *Archives of General Psychiatry* 48 [1991]: 1089–96.)

Psychological and environmental factors

There are far too many psychological and environmental factors to expound upon here, but the following are a few of the more common ones that have been noted concerning people with homosexual attractions. Of course, not every factor applies to every person. And in some cases, none of the factors apply.

1. *Problems in relationships with the same-sex parents.* Elizabeth Moberly discusses problems with same-sex parents experienced by those with homosexual attractions. She found that same-sex attraction can be the result of a deficit created by a poor relationship with the same-sex parent. This deficit can include complete absence of the same-sex parent, rejection, abuse, or a lack of approval or acceptance. The deficit creates a need for love and approval from the same sex in an attempt to compensate. Barriers of mistrust may exist, so the partner in a homosexual relationship may be loved and mistrusted at the same time. (*Homosexuality: A New Christian Ethic* [Greenwood, S. C.: Attie Press, 1983].)

Poor relationships with the same-sex parent evolve in a variety of ways. In an alarming number of cases, severe emotional, physical, or sexual abuse has occurred. Small acts of neglect or of withholding love might be less obvious but can often be damaging. For example, a boy might perceive his father as being detached or uninterested. In other cases, a father can seem very domineering and forceful, resulting in the boy's feeling timid and insecure. Relationship problems vary widely between a mother and daughter as well.

Talents and interests can also affect the child-parent relationship. A boy might enjoy dancing or other "less masculine" activities. That can seem strange or unacceptable to a father who enjoys sports and other traditionally male activities.

This is not to say that parents are necessarily at fault. Problems in the relationship are determined by the child's perception of what has happened. A child can perceive alienation and rejection when a parent has done his or her best to be loving and accepting. For instance, a mother may be suddenly forced to get a job to help make ends meet, and the daughter perceives that as abandonment.

More than one child from the same family might have homosexual attractions, but that is certainly not always the case. Differences in perceptions and reactions rather than in what actually occurred account, in part, for the differences in sexual orientation of children of the same parents.

2. *Problems with gender identity.* Some people have difficulty with their own masculinity or femininity, which is often the result of poor relationships with same-sex parents and same-sex peers. A boy gains confidence in his own masculinity from his father and friends. If he fails to bond with his father or peers, he might fail to identify with the masculine role. If a girl fails to identify with her mother, she may lack the confidence needed to feel secure in the feminine role. She might avoid feminine peer groups because she feels estranged from them. Her interests in activities that are not commonly considered feminine can contribute to feelings of alienation from many of her female peers.

Other circumstances, such as a family who moves frequently, can also affect the child's ability to form bonds with his or her peers, possibly affecting gender identity. That, in turn, can contribute to homosexual attractions.

3. Problems in relationships with an opposite-sex parent. Other contributing factors include difficulties in relationships with the parent of the opposite sex. Gerard van den Aardweg, a psychotherapist specializing in the study of homosexual attractions, reported that with many of his male clients, "the mother has been overly 'binding' in one way or another." He stated that such men transfer their attitudes concerning their mother "to other women as mother figures." It should be pointed out that the belief that all men with same-sex attraction had a domineering mother is a myth. Some certainly have had such a mother. But some men who struggle with same-sex attraction had wonderful relationships with their mothers.

The father influences a daughter's sense of her femininity. Absent or abusive fathers can exert a negative effect on the daughter's gender identity. Also, Dr. van den Aardweg notes that some "women with lesbian feelings were excessively attached to their fathers." (*Homosexuality and Hope* [Ann Arbor, Mich.: Servant Books, 1985], pp. 64–65, 69–71.)

Problems with parents of the opposite sex are just as varied and numerous as problems with the same-sex parent.

4. Abuse. Sexual, physical, or emotional abuse within or outside the family can contribute to homosexual attractions. If a woman has been abused by a man, a variety of problems can result, such as guilt, shame, fear, anger, hatred towards men, betrayal, helplessness, and/or the inability to form proper boundaries. Even though homosexual problems are often related to issues regarding relationships with the same sex, abuse from a man can keep a woman locked into homosexual behavior because she sees no viable alternative. She seeks the comfort, understanding, and safety that a relationship with another woman provides. Sometimes a woman who has been in an abusive or poor marriage will find herself attracted to another woman, even if she's never noticed such feelings before. She finds caring, concern, attention, and intimacy that involves more than a sexual relationship, causing her to feel her needs are finally being met.

Although boys may be victims of sexual abuse less often than girls, trauma associated with abuse can contribute to their same-sex attraction. One study reported that boys who were sexually victimized were seven times more likely to consider themselves homosexual or bisexual than those who were not victimized. (R. Johnson and D. Schrier, "Victimization of Boys," *Journal of Adolescent Health Care* 6 [1985]: 372–76.) If a boy was abused by an older boy or man, he might then seek sexual experiences with other males. Still less common is sexual abuse inflicted by women, but that can also affect the sexual orientation of both boys and girls. A counselor who works primarily with people struggling with same-sex attraction stated that abuse is a significant contributing factor. And the abuse can be difficult to identify because some may not even label sexual experiences that occurred with older children during their preteenage years as abuse. I know of several people, including me, who can identify sexual abuse as contributing to homosexual feelings.

Some, or none, of these biological and environmental factors may contribute to same-sex attraction in any one individual. There are some people who have homosexual feelings with no apparent causes. Those who are Church members may find that their struggles are a result of having homosexual feelings, not a cause of them. The guilt and lack of acceptance that accompany their feelings can often intensify the problem. Homosexual desires can also create doubt concerning the Church and Christ's doctrine. Such individuals find it difficult to gain freedom from those desires because they question the need or their ability to overcome them. Hence, the necessary faith cannot be exercised.

Most often needs or pains or deficits or traumas have contributed to homosexual feelings. Whether they appear to directly relate to the issue of same-sex attraction or not, they often do. Anything that creates unmet emotional needs can lead someone to try and satisfy those needs in a nontraditional way.

DEVELOPMENTAL PATTERNS OF HOMOSEXUAL ATTRACTIONS

Dr. William Consiglio states that homosexual desires develop when heterosexual desires become misdirected. He describes sexuality as a stream whose intended flow can be diverted by certain obstacles. The stream continues to flow, but it finds expression in other ways, such as homosexual desires and behavior.

Events that block and redirect sexual development usually occur during childhood or adolescence. Such events can include "unresolved family/parental relationships, the lack of good peer relationships, ineffective techniques for dealing with temptation, the lack of understanding about homosexuality, and others." Wounded emotions and difficulties with the opposite sex can also contribute. (*Homosexual No More* [Wheaton, Ill.: Victor Books, 1991], pp. 21–22.)

While they are growing up, boys go through a stage when they like boys instead of girls and vice versa. If development is altered by some event or situation at this point, attractions toward the same sex can intensify. Sexuality becomes misdirected as its natural course of progression through this phase is hindered. This misdirection can continue as the person matures to adulthood.

Joe Dallas, a Christian counselor who helps those seeking freedom from same-sex attraction, notes patterns in the formation of unmet emotional needs and explains how they often develop into homosexual attractions:

"1. A child's perception of his or her relationship to parents or significant others.

"2. A child's emotional response to those perceptions.

"3. Emotional needs arising from these perceptions and responses.

"4. The sexualization of those emotional needs."

He says that sexual needs are natural but that "sexualized needs, however, run a different course. These are emotional needs that are expressed indirectly through sexual activity, acted out through a sort of sexual pantomime. The needs themselves are usually legitimate, but the vehicle used to express them is not."

He continues, "What they're seeking—comfort, peace of mind, sexual pleasure—is not wrong in and of itself. It's the way they're seeking it that is unnatural. . . . I believe that we associate warm, positive feelings with sexual response long before we even know what sex is, because we associate our sexual organs with pleasure and comfort." (*Desires in Conflict* [Eugene, Oreg.: Harvest House, 1991], pp. 109–10.)

HETEROSEXUAL AND HOMOSEXUAL
ATTRACTIONS

Homosexual temptations are probably more common than we realize because some people do not wish to admit to them. Those who have tried to defend the acceptability of homosexual behavior—even insisting on a gospel acceptance—cite various proportions of the population who are presumably homosexual. Regardless of how common homosexual desires are, it is still not right to act on them. "There hath no temptation taken you but *such as is common to man: but God is faithful, who will not suffer you to be tempted above that ye are able; but will with the temptation also make a way to escape.*" (1 Corinthians 10:13; emphasis added.)

Homosexual attractions occur in a variety of intensities. For some, they are a driving force they find nearly impossible to resist. For others, feelings are only slight or temporary. Some may feel attracted to the opposite sex as well and choose either path.

Unfortunately, we often classify a person as either "homosexual" or "heterosexual." The Kinsey report, a highly debated study used most often to defend a homosexual lifestyle, states "it should be evident that one is not warranted in recognizing merely two types of individuals, heterosexual and homosexual, and that the characterization of the homosexual as a third sex fails to describe any actuality." (A. C. Kinsey, W. B. Pomeroy, and C. E. Martin, *Sexual Behavior in the Human Male* [Philadelphia: W. B. Saunders Co., 1948], p. 647.)

Labeling someone as anything other than a disciple of Christ can be damaging. A homosexual orientation is not so strictly determined that there can never be room for heterosexual feelings. Individuals who might consider themselves to be exclusively homosexual may later find themselves attracted to members of the opposite sex.

One man who had previously been homosexually oriented said, "One interesting thing is that, contrary to my expectations, there was never a focus in counseling to make me heterosexual but rather a focus on wholeness and healing. I was helped to more fully be myself. This may sound strange but as I developed appropriate relationships with men and women, I actually had some heterosexual, sexual feelings." (A. Dean Byrd, quoting "R," "Interview: An LDS

Reparative Therapy Approach for Male Homosexuality," *AMCAP Journal,* vol. 19, no. 1 [1993]: 103.)

Same-sex attraction does not make it impossible to become attracted toward the opposite sex. Some people have both attractions at the same time in their lives, confirming that the two types of attraction are not mutually exclusive.

Homosexual feelings do not mean that a person is homosexual. Some worry that because they've had a sexual experience with a member of the same sex and enjoyed it, they must be gay. Our bodies can enjoy sexual stimulation of any kind.

As for emotional attractions, it's common for women to relate better to other women, who often communicate on a deeper emotional level. Men tend to have more in common with other men. It should not come as any great surprise that members of the same sex often have a strong affinity for each other.

People frequently use the term "sexual preference." God does not ask us which sex we prefer, just as He does not ask those who struggle with alcoholism whether they prefer beer or wine over non-alcoholic beverages. "Satan strives to persuade us to live outside truth by rationalizing our actions as *the right of choice.*" (Richard G. Scott, "Healing Your Damaged Life," *Ensign,* Nov. 1992, p. 61; italics in original.)

To suggest that a homosexually oriented person can develop attractions toward the opposite sex infuriates some gay activists. Ironically, the very people who demand freedom to live whatever lifestyle they choose sometimes seek to discredit anyone who chooses to leave a homosexual way of life in search of heterosexual relationships.

Some people question whether people who have overcome same-sex attraction don't still have homosexual desires years later. If the answer is ever "yes, occasionally," the argument often ensues that they have not really changed.

Of course they've changed. They've managed consistently to avoid becoming sexually involved with members of the same sex, their desires to do so have greatly diminished, and they may have discovered attractions toward the opposite sex. Periodic temptations can continue for some time, but growth and change are certainly taking place.

The stance is sometimes taken that the slightest attraction toward the same sex indicates homosexuality, but that the development of attractions toward the opposite sex does not mean heterosexuality. It means latent homosexuality. Such reasoning is often used in an effort to destroy the belief that those who have lived a homosexual life can ever be happy living a heterosexual life.

Not everyone is physically or emotionally attracted to members of the opposite sex. Just as there are people who are not interested in becoming sexually involved with others of the same sex, so there are people who are not interested in becoming sexually involved with the opposite sex. But attractions toward the opposite sex can develop. Divine intervention may be needed to help uncover those desires. They may be buried under a lot of junk—traumatic events that have redirected sexual desires, genetic weakness, needs, pain, confusion, and anger. But certainly, if faith can move a mountain, it can move a pile of junk.

A change in brain structure according to change in thought patterns and behavior could very well be a scientific description of part of the miracle. However they happen, we do know miracles occur.

Carlfred Broderick, a well-known marriage counselor in the Church, makes several important observations about changes in the lives of men struggling with same-sex attraction. He observes how the Lord promises to intervene with help and knowledge when individual effort is put forth: "I have been impressed by how the Lord kept that promise [to help] with a series of young men who came to me with homosexual problems. At first, the possibility of ever being back on the track to the kingdom with a temple marriage and normal life-style seemed so far away to them that they could only contemplate it with despair. But step by step, they reached that goal. First, they learned how to deal with their negative feelings toward themselves. Gradually, they came to realize that they were of worth, whatever their life-style or afflictions. Next, they learned to conform to the commandments, even if only in a mechanical way. By the time they were living worthy to go to the temple, the Lord began to work a mighty change in their hearts. In each case, separately, they began to dream romantically about women and to discover the stirrings of attraction toward the opposite sex while losing feelings of attraction toward their own. Next, for each, the Lord raised up a good, patient woman who loved well and was easy to love in return. As each has said, 'This has been a series of miracles!' The key is in the word *series*. Each miracle built upon the one before it. By contrast, those who prayed, however fervently, for the miracle from the beginning, never received it, and if they were not willing to try the experiment of faith, step by step, they became bitter against God for his refusal to answer them and turned again to their former life-style." (Carlfred Broderick, *One Flesh, One Heart* [Salt Lake City: Deseret Book Co., 1986], pp. 79–80.)

This is not to say marriage is a cure for same-sex attraction. President Gordon B. Hinckley has said: "Marriage should not be viewed as a therapeutic step to solve problems such as homosexual inclinations or practices, which first should clearly be overcome with a firm and fixed determination." ("Reverence and Morality," *Ensign*, May 1987, p. 47.)

Attractions toward the opposite sex cannot be used as a measurement of progress towards freedom from homosexual desires. No one should be made to feel a failure or a sinner when opposite-sex attractions have not emerged.

The opposite of homosexual behavior is not heterosexual behavior; it is putting off the natural self and becoming like Christ.

THE NEED TO OVERCOME

Regardless of the causes of homosexual desires and behavior, we have been asked to overcome them and have been given the means whereby that can be accomplished. As George Q. Cannon stated: "If any of us are imperfect, it is our duty to pray for the gift that will make us perfect. . . . [The gifts of the Spirit] are intended for this purpose. No man ought to say, 'Oh, I cannot help this; it is my nature.' He is not justified in it, for the reason that God has promised to give strength to correct these things and to give gifts that will eradicate them." (*Gospel Truth*, sel. Jerreld L. Newquist, 2 vols. in 1 [Salt Lake City: Deseret Book Co., 1974, 1987], p. 155.)

The debate concerning the causes of same-sex attraction will, no doubt, continue. Perhaps the *Newsweek* article on homosexuality sums it up best: "'Something in the environment,' 'something biological'—the truth is, the nature-nurture argument is no longer as polarized as it once was. Scientists are beginning to realize there is a complex interplay between the two, still to be explored." ("Born or Bred?" p. 52.)

Research has little bearing on a spiritual discussion, except to increase understanding. I realize same-sex attraction is considered a problem mainly by those who are striving to live all of God's commandments. From a spiritual perspective, the fact that the American Psychiatric Association officially removed homosexual behavior from its list of mental disorders has no merit. Homosexual behavior might be considered normal, but that does not make it any less of a trial that needs to be overcome. Heterosexual relationships outside of marriage aren't on the list of mental disorders, either. Yet God's laws against adultery remain unchanged. It does not matter if the APA, the PTA, or the YMCA approves of homosexual behavior. The gospel works on a higher law.

OUR POTENTIAL TO BECOME GODS

The true, spirit self is not gay, because each of us has the potential to become gods. One characteristic of being a god is joining with another of the opposite sex. "Neither the man nor the woman were capable of filling the measure of their creation alone. The union of the two was required to complete man in the image of God." (Joseph Fielding Smith, *Doctrines of Salvation,* comp. Bruce R. McConkie, 3 vols. [Salt Lake City: Bookcraft, 1955], 2:70.)

To believe that we can become gods through a union between individuals of the same sex ignores scripture and modern revelation as well as physical evidence. Having the fulness of the restored gospel, we know that after the resurrection our spirits do not become ethereal nonentities, taking whatever form they please and joining with other spirit masses—"soul mates"—of any sex because there is no difference. Spirits and bodies become reunited in the image of our heavenly parents. The physical design of male and female bodies offers evidence that God created male and female to be joined and that only together can they have an eternal increase.

In the Doctrine and Covenants Christ tells us what it means to gain exaltation and have eternal lives—to become gods: "And again, verily I say unto you, if a man marry a wife by my word, which is my law, and by the new and everlasting covenant, . . . they shall pass by the angels . . . to their exaltation and glory . . . which glory shall be a fulness and a continuation of the seeds forever and ever. Then shall they be gods, because they have no end; therefore shall they be from everlasting to everlasting, because they continue; . . . For strait is the gate, and narrow the way that leadeth unto the exaltation and continuation of the lives, and few there be that find it." (D&C 132:19–22.)

Elder Bruce R. McConkie explains that "the word *eternal* . . . is one of the formal names of Deity and has been chosen by him as the particular name to identify the kind of life that he lives. . . . Thus: *God's life is eternal life; eternal life is God's life*—the expressions are synonymous." And "those who gain eternal life (exaltation) also gain *eternal lives*, meaning that in the resurrection they have *eternal 'increase,' 'a continuation of the seeds,' a 'continuation of the lives.'"* (*Mormon Doctrine*, 2d ed. [Salt Lake City: Bookcraft, 1966], pp. 237–38.)

Homosexual relationships prevent eternal increase. They are the opposite of God's life (eternal life); hence, they are truly ungodlike. Turning away from homosexual behavior does not mean denying the true self; it means denying "yourselves of all ungodliness." (Moroni 10:32.)

It is important for us to understand the nature of God and our own divine potential so we can become like Him. Joseph Smith said, "If men do not comprehend the character of God, they do not comprehend themselves." (*Teachings of the Prophet Joseph Smith*. sel. Joseph Fielding Smith [Salt Lake City: Deseret Book Co., 1976], p. 343.)

In two of the three temptations of Christ, Satan sought to cause Christ to question His true identity. "If thou be the Son of God. . . . " (Matthew 4:3.) Satan constantly strives to bring our identity into question as well. He says, "You are not a son or daughter of God. You do not have the capacity to become like Him and create worlds of your own. You are gay. You always have been, and you always will be."

Nevertheless, "knowing who we really are prepares us to use that knowledge to face temptations, to resist them, and then to act right-eously. Moses, knowing he was a son of God, . . . told Satan, 'Get thee hence.'" (Charles Didier, "Spiritual Security," *Ensign*, May 1987, p. 27.)

WE CANNOT CHANGE GOD'S LAWS

No matter how a person tries to justify sinful behavior, it is only "the doers of the law [who] shall be justified." (Romans 2:13.) Many have reinterpreted or excused parts of the Bible away in defense of homosexual behavior. Regardless of what people say, however, Heavenly Father's plan remains unchanged. In addition to scripture, we also have modern-day prophets to guide us. The restored gospel of Jesus Christ declares homosexual behavior to be sin. The First Presidency reconfirmed that doctrine in a November 1991 letter to the Church membership. The letter states: "Sexual relations are prop-er only between husband and wife appropriately expressed within the bonds of marriage. Any other sexual contact, including fornica-tion, adultery, and homosexual and lesbian behavior, is sinful."

I used to think that as soon as the Church got some "new, younger leaders" who really understand homosexual issues, the "rules" would change. I guess I thought they all sit around a big table and vote on whether or not a certain commandment should be rescinded or amended.

But the commandments, including those which declare homo-sexual behavior and the fostering of lustful feelings as sin, do not come from limited human understanding. They come from the mouth of God.

Elder Richard G. Scott states: "Our Heavenly Father gave us truth, some as statements of cause and effect. We call them com-mandments. They guide our life to happiness. He knew that Satan would try to persuade some to live without fixed standards in life so that decisions would be based on current circumstances, what appears convenient, or what provides the greatest personal return.

In this way, Satan removes the power of truth from one's life so he can take that soul captive." ("Healing Your Damaged Life," p. 61.)

And, as Elder L. Tom Perry says: "What He [the Lord] has declared to be sinful will always be sinful. Rest assured that when the so-called 'enlightened' doctrines of men contradict the holy scriptures, they will only bring heartache, disappointment, and destruction to the souls of mankind." ("Back to Gospel Basics," *Ensign,* May 1993, p. 92.)

The Lord will not suddenly change His mind and say homosexual behavior is OK. He will not approve of "homosexual marriage" because that is an oxymoron from an eternal perspective. "From the beginning of the creation God made them male and female. For this cause shall a man leave his father and mother, and cleave to his wife; and they twain shall be one flesh: so then they are no more twain, but one flesh." (Mark 10:6–8.)

Satan is the one who would have people wait for his concocted "approval from heaven concerning homosexual marriages." He seeks to have us put off the day of repentance rather than put off the natural self.

No matter how much people want to change the law or excuse it away, it can't be done. God is eternal, and so are His truths. "We can scoff at sacred things, rationalize our behavior, spout our own ideas, agree or disagree, but it doesn't change anything. We cannot alter God's laws, his truth." (Elaine Cannon, "Agency and Accountability," *Ensign,* Nov. 1983, p. 88.)

SATAN DECEIVES THROUGH FALSE "PERSONAL REVELATION"

It was difficult for me to believe Satan had any part in homosexual relationships because I found them to be full of love. I was involved with good, caring people. I forgot that good, caring people can still be enticed by the adversary, and so could I.

Because homosexual relationships seemed full of love, I thought they were "light" and spiritually correct: for "whatsoever is light, is good." (Alma 32:35.) But the adversary can mimic even light. "Satan himself is transformed into an angel of light." (2 Corinthians 11:14.)

Satan also imitates personal revelation. Christ says, "I will tell you in your mind and in your heart, by the Holy Ghost." (D&C 8:2.) Satan seeks to deceive us through those same two channels. There are very convincing arguments—telling us in our minds—that homosexual behavior is normal, acceptable unto the Lord, and irresistible. A strong message comes rushing through the heart—the emotions—"confirming" that something so fulfilling must somehow be "spiritually correct."

"Be ever on guard lest you be deceived by inspiration from an unworthy source. You can be given false spiritual messages. . . .

"The spiritual part of us and the emotional part of us are so closely linked that it is possible to mistake an emotional impulse for something spiritual." (Boyd K. Packer, "Candle of the Lord," *Ensign,* Jan. 1983, pp. 56–57.)

I think sometimes we half expect Satan to have a pointed tail and horns and to run around waving a pitchfork saying, "Hey look, it's me. The devil is here with a message just for you." He is seldom so obvious. He creates well-crafted counterfeits, facsimiles that bear an incredible likeness to the real thing. We think we are so clever and can spot him a mile off. Well, Satan has been busy fooling people, even geniuses and those with honest hearts, for a long time. We do not always recognize him. He does not have a pointed tail and horns.

Satan is quite adept at convincing people his way is "spiritually correct." Before life on earth began, he managed to deceive a third of the hosts of heaven and convince them that his way was the right way.

It wasn't until I had removed myself from homosexual relationships and worked through many of my feelings that I realized the apparent rightness of homosexual relationships was actually Satan's masterfully created counterfeit. As C. S. Lewis says, "You can see mistakes in arithmetic when your mind is working properly: while you are making them you cannot see them." (*Mere Christianity* [New York: Macmillan, 1943], p. 87.)

"THIS IS GENUINE LOVE"

Another way in which I convinced myself (with Satan's help) that homosexual relationships were right was by saying, "Certainly Christ would not disapprove of love between two people. It's genuine, Christlike love. How could He object?" He objects when love results in sin, which love is not the pure and undefiled love of Christ.

We have been warned against putting any love before Him. "For I am come to set a man at variance against his father, and the daughter against her mother, and the daughter in law against her mother in law. And a man's foes shall be they of his own household. He that loveth father or mother [or lover] more than me is not worthy of me: and he that loveth son or daughter more than me is not worthy of me. And he that taketh not his cross, and followeth after me, is not worthy of me. He that findeth his life shall lose it: and he that loseth his life for my sake shall find it." (Matthew 10:35–39.)

To find and keep a homosexual life is to lose eternal life with Christ. To give up that homosexual life for Christ's sake is to find eternal life. We choose which course we will take.

THE ETERNAL PERSPECTIVE

I realize there are at least two sides to this debate. For every point I have made someone can, and most likely will, present convincing arguments to the contrary. There are those who cleverly present the philosophy and psychology of the world with scripture mixed in.

From the perspective of the restored gospel, it comes down to these eternal truths. The Lord has declared that homosexual behavior and consciously fostering lustful feelings are sin. It was, is, and always will be Christ's mission "to bring to pass the immortality and eternal life" of each one of us. (Moses 1:39.) Prerequisites for gaining eternal life and exaltation are described by the Savior in the Doctrine and Covenants as the union of man and woman, sealed by and abiding by the new and everlasting covenant, having a continuation of the seeds forever and ever. (D&C 132.) Intellectual arguments to the contrary—including scripture or not—represent the world's view.

Actually, "intellectual arguments" contrary to the commandments should be called "knowledgeable arguments." As President
Joseph F. Smith said, "I know men who have knowledge, who
understand the principles of the Gospel, perhaps as well as you do,
who are brilliant, but who lack the essential qualification of pure
intelligence. They will not accept and render obedience thereto. Pure
intelligence comprises not only knowledge, but also the power to
properly apply that knowledge." (*Gospel Doctrine* [Salt Lake City:
Deseret Book Co., 1939], p. 58.)

For years, eternal Truth was hidden from my view. Pain, anger,
guilt, confusion, and doubt presented a false identity and smothered
my true one. Sparks of divinity would flash, quickly doused by the
weakness of my own mortal condition. Just as soon as I felt a call to
something greater, I became painfully aware of something lesser.

Today, the constant awareness of my own divine potential far
outweighs the intermittent awareness of my past. I don't feel I am
"gay." I don't feel I'm "denying myself" or "living a lie." I am living
the greatest Truth of all. Deep within I have a sense of who I am and
who I can become. Because of my past, some people may insist that
I'm a latent homosexual. I lay claim to latent divinity.

CHAPTER 4

THE GREAT I AM

I have encountered much opposition while writing this book. Apparently Satan hasn't been pleased. His frontal attacks have backfired, however, because they've given me a much greater awareness of spiritual matters in general and of the power of Jesus Christ in particular.

In winning this battle, my spiritual eyesight has been improved. It has been for me much as it was for the servant of Elisha who saw the Syrian armies massed against Israel. Elisha told him, "Fear not: for they that be with us are more than they that be with them." Then he prayed that the servant's eyes could be opened so that he could see "the mountain was full of horses and chariots of fire round about Elisha." (2 Kings 6:16–17.)

Satan has promoted misunderstanding throughout the body of the Church on both sides of the issue of homosexual attractions, causing a falling-out when there desperately needs to be a falling-in of God's army. Satan has confused the issue long enough. It's time to dismiss him and his arguments. "In the name of the Only Begotten, depart hence, Satan." (Moses 1:21.)

During these last days, the adversary has been trying to convince people that all kinds of trials and weaknesses are permanent. "I am anorexic." "I'm an alcoholic." "I am weak." "I am gay." And all the while stands before us and within us the Great I Am—calling us to something beyond our mortal condition. He reminds us that we were with Him long before we were with the world. He asks us to become as He is, "even as I Am." (3 Nephi 27:27.)

No one is permanently trapped. As Truman Madsen states, "Modern man is not imprisoned in his body but imprisoned in a set of distortions of it. Man, not God, has turned his body into a perpetual torture chamber. . . . The redeeming truth is that Jesus Christ lived and died not only to heal, lift, and fulfill all men but *all of man*—intelligence, spirit, and body. And He exemplified magnificently the possible final outcome." ("The Mind and the Body," *Instructor,* Sept. 1964, p. 365.)

Christ is mighty to lift us above any earthly trial or unrighteous desire. But sometimes the natural part of us shouts loudly, drowning out the still small voice. We no longer listen to Christ's urgent pleas; rather, we listen to our own.

Soon, the heavens seem like brass, and calls from above sound shrill, as if from a discordant brass section in a bad junior high band. We cannot believe such an awful racket could actually be coming from heaven. It creates an unbearable disharmony with our feelings and needs. We become erroneously convinced that it's out-of-tune Church leaders creating the discord. We mistake the Lord's commandments for squawks from without instead of a divine beckoning from within.

Gradually the beckoning becomes despised. We fight to rid ourselves of a testimony that once had the strength of two thousand stripling warriors. Christ's weapons are buried in the hope of finding peace. He is, at times, even seen as the enemy. "Why won't He let me find peace in the only way I can?"

Satan insists that the years of turmoil will never go away, that the struggle will always be a struggle. But it is winning the battle that promises peace. Surrendering means only that the enemy is in control. He fabricates a poor semblance of peace as we attempt to end the conflict simply by saying there is no conflict.

The relief from the turmoil seems like peace in comparison to the battle—but only in comparison. True peace cannot be had with the enemy, for the enemy is Satan. Christ is our Advocate. A testimony of Him can become a powerful weapon rather than a hindrance. Learning to value that despised testimony can provide great strength.

Jesus Christ wants to build us up. He loves us, no matter where we are or what we're doing. He wants us to be His. He knows how difficult the battle is, and He's prepared to die for us. In truth, He already has.

It might seem as though "the Church" doesn't understand what it's like to struggle with same-sex attraction. Christ does understand, and He is at the head of The Church of Jesus Christ of Latter-day Saints. He comprehends all things because He went below all things. One reason He descended below all things was so that He could with full compassion help each of us with each of our struggles: "And he shall go forth, *suffering pains and afflictions and temptations of every kind*; and this that the word might be fulfilled which saith he will take upon him the pains and the sicknesses of his people . . . and he will take upon him their infirmities, that his bowels may be filled with mercy, according to the flesh, that he may know according to the flesh how to succor his people according to their infirmities." (Alma 7:11–12; emphasis added.)

Christ's life and atonement extend not only to those who are sinning but to those who suffer pains, afflictions, infirmities, and temptations of every kind. Those who have suffered abuse, neglect or mistreatment—whatever the weakness or trial—can find healing through the Savior, Jesus Christ.

After being miraculously cured of a physical illness, Elder Gene R. Cook said, "I testify that the Lord, through His grace, can continually assist us in our daily lives and in our physical and mental sickness, pain, transgressions, and even in all of our infirmities." ("Receiving Divine Assistance through the Grace of the Lord," *Ensign*, May 1993, p. 80.)

GRACE

"Yea, come unto Christ, and be perfected in him, and deny yourselves of all ungodliness; and if ye shall deny yourselves of all ungodliness, and love God with all your might, mind and strength, then is his grace sufficient for you, that by his grace ye may be perfect in Christ." (Moroni 10:32.)

Grace is a "divine means of help or strength, given through the bounteous mercy and love of Jesus Christ." It's how individuals "receive strength and assistance to do good works that they otherwise would not be able to maintain if left to their own means. This grace is an *enabling power* that allows men and women to lay hold on eternal life and exaltation after they have expended their own best efforts." ("Grace," LDS Bible Dictionary, p. 697; emphasis added.)

With God all things are possible. And "with God" means with grace, or with divine assistance. Grace is an "enabling power," enabling us to do things we could not do alone.

It would be impossible for me to maintain a life free from homosexual behavior and desires, not to mention other desires to sin, without grace. I have learned to lean on Jesus Christ at all times and in all things, and that has given me greater power—His power. "And [Jesus] said unto me, My grace is sufficient for thee: for my strength is made perfect in weakness. Most gladly therefore will I rather glory in my infirmities, that the power of Christ may rest upon me." (2 Corinthians 12:9.)

Satan would have us believe we have to be clean and worthy before we can receive divine help, as if we could become clean and worthy without Christ's assistance. "Christ Jesus came into the world to save sinners" (1 Timothy 1:15), not the perfect people we imagine exist.

"We should have great hope in knowing, however unworthy we may feel or weak we may be, *that if we will do all we can,* [Jesus Christ] will come to our aid and provide for us whatever we may lack." ("Receiving Divine Assistance through the Grace of the Lord," p. 80; italics in original.)

Christ asks us to give our all, to try as hard as we can to receive divine help. Even if a person can avoid an act of sin for only one day—and it takes all of his or her effort to do so—that is sufficient to receive more grace. For "it is by grace that we are saved, after all we can do." (2 Nephi 25:23.) There is a constant exchange of grace and works, so that actually we are saved by grace before, during, and after all we can do.

Sometimes we think we must meet Christ somewhere along the way when, in reality, He *is* the Way. Christ is the beginning. He is also the process—the Way. And He is our means of exaltation. He is

"Jesus Christ, the Great I AM, Alpha and Omega, the beginning and the end." (D&C 38:1.)

COMING UNTO THE GREAT I AM

The process of becoming like Christ, the Great I Am, is a gradual one that requires grace every step of the way. As the Prophet Joseph Smith said: "Here, then, is eternal life—to know the only wise and true God; and you have got to learn how to be Gods yourselves, . . . the same as all Gods have done before you, namely, by going from one small degree to another, and from a small capacity to a great one; from grace to grace." (*Teachings of the Prophet Joseph Smith,* sel. Joseph Fielding Smith [Salt Lake City: Deseret Book Co., 1938], pp. 346–47.)

Coming unto the Great I Am was gradual even for Christ himself. "Once a meek and lowly Lamb, / Now the Lord, the great I Am." ("Jesus, Once of Humble Birth," *Hymns of The Church of Jesus Christ of Latter-day Saints* [Salt Lake City: The Church of Jesus Christ of Latter-day Saints, 1985], no. 196.)

John, bearing record of Jesus, states: "And he received not of the fulness at first, but continued from grace to grace, until he received a fulness." Christ promises us, "For if you keep my commandments you shall receive of his fulness, and be glorified in me as I am in the Father; therefore, I say unto you, you shall receive grace for grace." (D&C 93:13, 20.)

Christ's grace is sufficient for everyone to come unto Him. "The sanctifying grace of the Savior Jesus Christ is the source of an entire cluster of blessings and powers. The Atonement not only atones for our sins and compensates for our inadequacies, it is also the source of spiritual endowments that develop and ultimately transform our very nature." (Bruce C. Hafen, *The Broken Heart* [Salt Lake City: Deseret Book Co., 1989], p. 175.)

"Transform our very nature" does not mean that everything about us is changed. Gradually our true selves emerge as we become like Christ. It happens grace for grace, glory to glory. "But we all, with open face beholding as in a glass the glory of the Lord, are changed into the same image from glory to glory, even as by the Spirit of the Lord." (2 Corinthians 3:18.) We must look with an eye single to God's glory to see Christ for who He truly is, and to see ourselves for who we truly are. Looking to Him, we become as He is.

With a veil, it's not always easy to see clearly. Our vision becomes muddy. We cannot see through the murk of mortal circumstance, and "we see through a glass, darkly." (1 Corinthians 13:12.)

Committing sin or questioning God's commandments makes the picture fuzzy. Instead of seeing our true selves, we see our natural selves. "For if any be a hearer of the word, and not a doer, he is like unto a man beholding his natural face in a glass: For he beholdeth himself, and goeth his way, and straightway forgetteth what manner of man he was." (James 1:23–24.) And "what manner of men ought ye to be? Verily I say unto you, even as I am." (3 Nephi 27: 27.)

When I attempted to free myself from homosexual desires and behavior, I questioned many things. But there were two things I could never deny: the Book of Mormon is the word of God, and Jesus is the Christ.

Even though I had faith in Christ, I'd never really felt His presence. Nor did I feel worthy of it. He never seemed very real to me. I knew He walked around on the dusty roads of Nazareth and Jerusalem and all those other biblical places some two thousand years ago. I knew He went about healing those who believed He could, way back then. I knew people touched His robe and washed His feet and anointed His head. They felt the wounds in His hands and side.

But what about me in the twentieth century? I would pray and wait. Nothing would happen. Everything seemed like a stupor of thought. The spiritual did not seem real. Nevertheless, as I turned away from sin and turned toward Christ, gradually—grace for grace, year upon year—things changed. Now, the spiritual is the most tangible aspect of my life.

Not only did Jesus walk the dusty roads of Palestine but He has walked the sandy shores of the Pacific Ocean with me. I have touched His robe, for He has taken my crippled childhood and healed it. His "light is come into [my] world." I have fallen asleep, encircled "in the arms of [His] love." I have washed His feet by helping "the least of these." I talk of Christ, I rejoice in Christ, and I preach of Christ. I have received confirming witness after confirming witness. I know

He lived and died and lives again for each one of us. He is my Exemplar, my King, my Redeemer, my Savior, my God, and my Friend.

It is "upon the rock of our Redeemer, who is Christ, the Son of God, that ye must build your foundation; that when the devil shall send forth his mighty winds, yea, his shafts in the whirlwind, yea, when all his hail and his mighty storm shall beat upon you, it shall have no power over you . . . because of the rock upon which ye are built." (Helaman 5:12.)

The winds will blow, and the torrential rains will come. Satan will create storms to block the light. But those who know the Truth and with whom the Spirit has not ceased to strive can never completely believe the lies. Deep down inside is the knowledge of greater things. There is an eternal stirring, like an anxious child waiting at the window for the rain to stop so he can run out to play.

Spiritual feelings can nag and create incredible discomfort. They may seem, in times of struggling with temptation and sin, to be a curse, a nemesis. The truth is, there is no greater Friend. The stirring is Jesus Christ. It is the light of Christ, the hope in Christ, the Spirit of Christ. Be it ever so dim or so bright, it dissipates the darkness and illuminates the Truth.

Dark voices may echo the lie "I am gay," but that message is from the father of all lies. "Hearken and listen to the voice of him who is from all eternity to all eternity, the Great I AM, even Jesus Christ— The light and the life of the world; a light which shineth in darkness and the darkness comprehendeth it not." (D&C 39:1–2.) He is the light that calls us from within and above to become, not as we will, but as "I AM."

CHAPTER 5

HOPE—
Light Amidst Darkness

Hope flickers in the darkness.
I can feel failure's baited breath at my back,
Blowing at the Light
I stoop hunched over to protect.

Heavenly Father, please,
I can't stay this way much longer.

As the battle was raging, darkness was my greatest enemy. "For we wrestle not against flesh and blood, but against principalities, against powers, against the rulers of the darkness of this world." (Ephesians 6:12.) When life was at its worst, it was always hope that first pierced the blackness.

Hope is where anyone struggling to find freedom from same-sex attraction can begin. Hope that freedom is possible. Hope that Christ is near and willing to do all He has promised to do. Hope that the future will bring a permanent reprieve from the past and the present.

THE LIGHT OF HOPE

Using loneliness, depression, and confusion, Satan and his band of not-so-merry men concocted a darkness that seemed impossible for me to endure. It was so thick it blocked the Light from the Son. Without that Light my life seemed hopeless.

A lack of hope means a lack of light, for hope is light. "Wherefore, ye must press forward with a steadfastness in Christ, having a perfect brightness of hope." (2 Nephi 31:20.)

Satan does everything in his power to smother the light of hope, because without it people lose the determination to keep trying. On the other hand, hope for winning a spiritual battle enlists the greatest power within each of us and within the universe—the light of hope, or the light of Christ.

For instance, David had great hope and faith that Goliath could be defeated, regardless of the odds. "Then said David to the Philistine, Thou comest to me with a sword, and with a spear, and with a shield: but I come to thee in the name of the Lord of hosts, the God of the armies of Israel, whom thou hast defied." (1 Samuel 17:45.)

When I first attempted to leave homosexual relationships, I did not know of anyone who had won the battle I was fighting. All I knew was that a mighty giant stood before me with sword and spear and shield. There I stood, without my shield of faith or my sword of truth, hardly realizing those weapons were available to me and to anyone who seeks them.

How could I win such a battle? Everyone else I knew had fled, and not because they were cowards. The confrontation had left them battered and broken. Several of my friends had attempted to leave homosexual relationships because of the gospel and had given up because they refused to feel miserable, or at best unfulfilled, the rest of their lives. The worldly message was, "Don't be foolish! There is no hope for change. Be free to express your own homosexual feelings." As in times of old, voices questioned, "O ye that are bound down under a foolish and a vain hope, why do ye yoke yourselves with such foolish things?" (Alma 30:13.)

Satan offered artificial light, sometimes in the form of false hope. "Oh, no need to worry, my dear friend. The leaders of the Church are mistaken. Don't feel dark and depressed. There is hope."

I had met with failure so many times before that this false hope was easier to believe than the hope for freedom from same-sex attraction. Hope in Christ requires "hope for those things which they have not seen." (Ether 12:8.) Hope for the natural self comes from things that are seen with natural eyes. I had proof that could be seen, evidence of my own failures and those of others, that caused me to believe that finding freedom was impossible and unnecessary.

The night I met with the bishop to tell him I was leaving the Church for Tracy, my outlook changed. The Spirit withdrew from me, bearing witness of the true darkness I would encounter if I continued in a homosexual relationship. I cannot explain the intensity of that darkness. It came from without and from within—all at once. I felt like Jonah being swallowed up by a great fish after he sought to hide from the presence of the Lord. "The waters compassed me about, even to the soul: the depth closed me round about, the weeds were wrapped about my head. I went down to the bottoms of the mountains; the earth with her bars was about me for ever." (Jonah 2:5–6.)

The darkness that came when the Lord withdrew His Spirit testified to me what true darkness was. I had not noticed the light of Christ until it was removed. Shortly after the truest of all darknesses consumed me, a light began to flicker. I received a witness that Christ is the Way and the Light for the Way. "For the commandment is a lamp; and the law is light; and reproofs of instruction are the way of life." (Proverbs 6:23.)

He reproved me "betimes with sharpness, . . . and then [showed] forth afterwards an increase of love." (D&C 121:43.) After all light was removed, Christ mercifully and lovingly called me forward, beckoning me to follow His Light. "I am the light of the world: he that followeth me shall not walk in darkness, but shall have the light of life." (John 8:12.) "Come follow me."

THE POWER TO OVERCOME DARKNESS

My unhappiness and depression came about because circumstances and events, such as the abuse and subsequent confusion and guilt, blocked the light of Christ from within and from above. Later I allowed the weaknesses and desires of my natural self to block the light I so desperately needed. Light and love bring joy. Darkness brings misery.

Negative feelings create a sort of solar eclipse that blocks the Light from the Son. This darkness can bring depression, pain, and a lack of hope. "Hope deferred maketh the heart sick." (Proverbs 13:12.)

I once saw an ad promoting mental health. It was a solid page of black ink with small, white letters in the middle that read something like "Whoever called it the 'blues' never suffered from depression." My life was like that ad. The worst of times were dark, even black. They were hopeless.

I felt as though a dark void had drained life out of me. I felt empty and alone. This void, or "hole in the soul," as it has been called, is felt by many who struggle with same-sex attraction.

In *Breaking the Cycle of Compulsive Behavior*, Martha and John Beck discuss their study of Church members who dealt with various self-destructive behaviors. The people they interviewed talked about that same void. They "described these feelings [of isolation] as loneliness, a sense of having been abandoned, the belief that they were unworthy or incapable of being loved, or as a 'homesickness for heaven.' . . . Whatever its cause, the behavioral addicts we interviewed expressed an almost universal feeling that a void existed within them. Although they described the void in different words, all agreed that it was an emptiness that cried out to be filled.

"In the case of the behavioral addicts, each individual had stumbled across some activity that did not fill this void, yet for a time produced physical or emotional sensations strong enough to block the person's awareness of the feelings of isolation." (Salt Lake City: Deseret Book Co., 1990, pp. 15–17.)

In my case, I sought immediately to fill the void with homosexual relationships and alcohol. Satan tempted me with his artificial light, offering immediate relief that could be had at the flick of a switch rather than through being patient in my afflictions. I had to learn to endure the pain and darkness of the void, even when I was never quite sure I could find freedom. Emphasizing the faith we need to have in Jesus' power to illuminate our way, President Harold B. Lee said, "You must learn to walk to the edge of the light, and then a few steps into the darkness, then the light will appear and show the way before you." (Quoted by Boyd K. Packer, "The Edge of the Light," address delivered at Brigham Young University, Provo, Utah, 4 Mar. 1990.)

COMMANDMENTS BRING HOPE

The commandments against homosexual behavior and lustful desires are designed to bring hope, or light, not despair. "For the word of the Lord is truth, and whatsoever is truth is light, and whatsoever is light is Spirit, even the Spirit of Jesus Christ." (D&C 84:45.)

We are promised that all sin can be overcome. "The Lord giveth no commandments unto the children of men, save he shall prepare a way for them that they may accomplish the thing which he commandeth them." (1 Nephi 3:7.) The eternal truth that homosexual behavior is sin provides hope that such behavior and desires can indeed be overcome and that eternal life is attainable for each one of us. As I truly began to believe that, it brought me hope.

Another commandment that eventually brought me hope is one that brought me discouragement at first: "Whosoever looketh on a woman to lust after her" is committing sin. (Matthew 5:28.) Because lusting after a person is sin, it can be overcome—in this life. I came to understand that I wouldn't have to "lust after" women forever, that the power of God brings freedom from the continual longing for homosexual relationships. I wouldn't have to spend the rest of my life constantly trying to resist.

THE LIGHT OF CHRIST

Hope is the light of Christ, and each of us is born with that light. "I am the true light that lighteth every man that cometh into the world." (D&C 93:2.)

Part of us is already like Christ. We have life because of His light. "Then shall ye know . . . that I am the true light that is in you, and that you are in me; otherwise ye could not abound." (D&C 88:50.) Christ is powerful. Realizing that He is a permanent part of us brings great power from within.

Science has discovered that light is a form of energy and that it is also necessary for life. Our latter-day scriptures tell us: "This is the light of Christ. As also he is in the sun, and the light of the sun, and the power thereof by which it was made." (D&C 88:7.)

Hope—the light of Christ—can produce the energy needed to keep trying. Christ is "the life and the light of the world." He is "the light which is in all things, which giveth life to all things, which is the law by which all things are governed, even the power of God who sitteth upon his throne." (D&C 88:13.)

I always thought I was weak because I kept succumbing to temptation. Without recognizing the light of Christ from within and from above, I *was* weak. But with His power, I could overcome all things. The very fact that I kept battling same-sex attraction demonstrated strength.

"For it must needs be, that there is an opposition in all things." (2 Nephi 2:11.) Yes, same-sex desires are extremely powerful, but so are the people battling them. If that were not so, there would be no contest. It takes a strong, determined person to go up against homosexual desires.

At a conference for Mormons seeking freedom from same-sex attraction, a man powerfully testified—and the Spirit bore witness—that although he had fallen again recently, he was still fighting to overcome. Despite his setbacks, he continued to have hope. He reminded me of a prizefighter who had been beaten and bruised and knocked down several times. But the count never reached "ten." I've seen some of those boxers emerge as champions. They're bleeding and swollen, and you think, "Surely someone is going to call this fight. Look at that poor guy." And just as you're feeling sorry for him, he charges his opponent with the strength of ten men, and the next thing you know, the referee is holding the fighter's glove in the air and declaring him the winner. "Where on earth did he get that strength?"

"I will be on your right hand and on your left, and my Spirit shall be in your hearts, and mine angels round about you, to bear you up." (D&C 84:88.) The determination to continue fighting against same-sex attraction is not an earthly strength. It comes from the light of Christ within, supplemented by the light of Christ from above. It is the greatest power in this life because it *is* life.

President David O. McKay taught that "man is a spiritual being, a soul, and at some period of his life everyone is possessed with an irresistible desire to know his relationship to the Infinite. . . . There is something within him which urges him to rise above himself, to control his environment, to master the body and all things physical and live in a higher and more beautiful world." (*True to the Faith*, comp. Llewellyn R. McKay [Salt Lake City: Bookcraft, 1966], p. 244.)

Each of us has the power to overcome darkness. It is not society's norms or parental upbringing or any other earthly force that keeps a person fighting against homosexual desires. It is the light of Christ. "Light and truth forsake that evil one." (D&C 93:37.)

THE LIGHT OF TRUTH

We all began as the light of truth. It is an integral part of us. "Man was also in the beginning with God. Intelligence, or the light of truth, was not created or made, neither indeed can be." (D&C 93:29.) The true self embodies that light. It has the power and freedom to act. The scripture continues, "All truth is independent in that sphere in which God has placed it, to act for itself, as all intelligence [or light of truth] also; otherwise there is no existence. Behold, here is the agency of man, and here is the condemnation of man; because that which was from the beginning is plainly manifest unto them, and they receive not the light." (D&C 93:30–31.)

Light can be taken away by Satan, by sins committed against us, and by sins we commit. "That wicked one cometh and taketh away light and truth, through disobedience, from the children of men, and because of the tradition of their fathers." (D&C 93:39.)

But our true self is able "to act for itself." The body may have been "acted upon" (2 Nephi 2:14) by Satan, past trauma, sin, confusion, doubt, and the "traditions of their fathers." The adversary coaxes people to abuse or condemn or love conditionally in order to smother the light of Christ in others. Regardless of Satan's efforts to "act upon" us, the true self still has the power to act. As we work through problems, we gain more and more freedom to act.

I am able to recall much of my struggle, yet, I cannot recall the ominous darkness and depression. I can talk about it, but it is mostly on an intellectual level. I know it was there. I can see myself in despair, wanting to commit suicide. But I cannot recall the darkness. That is because the light of Christ has filled the void within me. "Which light proceedeth forth from the presence of God to fill the immensity of space." (D&C 88:12.)

My story and the stories of others that I have included in Appendix A, are intended to provide hope. Many other people, inside and outside the Church, have gained freedom from same-sex attraction. For example, Exodus is a Christian ministry devoted to this cause, and many of those involved have found freedom through Christ.

It is Jesus Christ who takes our hand when we begin to sink in despair, enabling us to rise above our circumstance and cross the void. As He told Peter before he sought to walk across the deep waters, "Be of good cheer; it is I; be not afraid." (Matthew 14:27.)

We must look to the Savior, not to the challenges that beset us. "And if your eye be single to my glory, your whole bodies shall be filled with light, and there shall be no darkness in you; and that body which is filled with light comprehendeth all things." (D&C 88:66.)

Christ defies the ways of the world. Others might say there is no hope for freedom. But I bear witness that with Christ there is hope. I seek to bring "to light all the hidden things of darkness, wherein [I] know them." (D&C 123:13.) Satan is not the god of this world; he only pretends to be.

Everyone has access to power and light through the One who rebuked the wind and the sea. He is mightier than all the earth, then why not mightier than same-sex attraction?

I was once as consumed in darkness as I could be without killing myself. Now I am consumed with light. I was once completely dependent upon homosexual relationships for my happiness. Now I am completely independent of them. The light of truth has set me free.

CHAPTER 6

FAITH—
The Power to Put Off the Natural Self

How is it that ye can attain unto faith, save ye shall have hope? And . . . ye shall have hope through the atonement of Christ and the power of his resurrection, to be raised unto life eternal, and this because of your faith in him according to the promise. Wherefore, if a man have faith he must needs have hope; for without faith there cannot be any hope." (Moroni 7:40–42.)

During the beginning of my struggle, the occasional flicker of hope brought faith in a source of Light. I had the feeling that perhaps Christ was real and close by. As my faith in Christ increased, it brought greater hope that His promise of freedom from the bondage of sin could be fulfilled.

At first I did not have enough hope and faith to produce the power necessary to resist temptation. Comfort and love and fulfillment were what I was seeking. Sometimes I needed those things so desperately that I'd take them in whatever immediate way I could. I hungered and thirsted after them. Rather than finding them through righteousness, which involved a trial of my faith over time, I often sought to be satiated immediately and chose from Satan's vast selection of junk food.

Christ knew the woman at the well was thirsting after something. It was not merely to demonstrate His ominscience that Jesus disclosed to the woman the circumstances of her life. He knew that she was living with a man who was not her husband and that there had been five husbands previously. In so saying, the Savior was identifying the source of her thirst.

Just how great a void was she trying to fill in her life? "The woman saith unto him, Sir, thou hast nothing to draw with, and the well is deep: from whence then hast thou that living water?" Then "Jesus answered and said unto her, Whosoever drinketh of this water shall thirst again: but whosoever drinketh of the water that I shall give him shall never thirst; but the water that I shall give him shall be in him a well of water springing up into everlasting life." (John 4:11, 13–14.)

No matter how great the void, how deep the well, how desperate the hunger and thirst, Jesus Christ can fill it far beyond mortal capacity. We must not seek the ways of the world to satisfy; rather, we should "feast upon that which perisheth not, neither can be corrupted, and let your soul delight in fatness. . . . Let your hearts rejoice." (2 Nephi 9:51–52.) We are told: "And blessed are all they who do hunger and thirst after righteousness, for they shall be filled with the Holy Ghost." (3 Nephi 12:6.)

As He did with the woman at the well, Christ warns us not to seek fulfillment from Satan's counterfeits. They may satisfy for a time, but such satisfaction is only an illusion. It "shall be as a dream of a night vision; yea, it shall be unto them, even as unto a hungry man which dreameth, and behold he eateth but he awaketh and his soul is empty; or like unto a thirsty man which dreameth, and behold he drinketh but he awaketh and behold he is faint, and his soul hath appetite." (2 Nephi 27:3.)

Alma counsels us to "awake and arouse your faculties, even to an experiment upon my words, and exercise a particle of faith, yea, even if ye can no more than desire to believe, let this desire work in you, even until ye believe in a manner that ye can give place for a portion of my words." (Alma 32:27.)

He then gives us what I believe is the most practical description of obtaining faith that can be found in the scriptures. First he discusses the necessity of desiring to believe. Even the person continually involved in homosexual behavior can begin with hope that it is possible to overcome homosexual desires and actions. The desire to believe starts to replace, ever so slightly, the desires to stay in homosexual relationships. "Let this desire work in you, even until ye believe in a manner that ye can give place for a portion of my words. Now, we will compare the word unto a seed. Now, if ye give place, that a seed may be planted in your heart, behold, if it be a true seed, or a good seed, if ye do not cast it out by your unbelief, that ye will resist the Spirit of the Lord, behold, it will begin to swell within your breasts." (Alma 32:27–28.)

In other words, making room for the desire to overcome and refusing to let go of the belief that change is possible can diminish doubt. Joseph Smith taught: "For doubt and faith do not exist in the same person at the same time; so that persons whose minds are under doubts and fears cannot have unshaken confidence; and where unshaken confidence is not there faith is weak." (*Lectures on Faith,* 6:12.)

Holding to the belief that freedom is possible and refusing to cast it out because of doubt will "enlarge [your] soul; yea, it beginneth to enlighten [your] understanding, yea, it beginneth to be delicious to [you]. . . . nevertheless it hath not grown up to a perfect knowledge."

The enlarging of the soul and the enlightening of understanding confirm hope and faith, but it happens according to God's timing. Faith is tried and exercised through spiritual stretching.

I received rewards of my faith as I reached various levels of progression. The confirmation of faith was never so strong that it interfered with my agency. I was not given a "perfect knowledge," but each confirmation became more and more obvious and undeniable. I would be lifted above my circumstances and allowed samplings of what heaven had to offer, and then I would be set back down to continue my journey.

At times, when I wasn't being careful, I would try to explain away the spiritual confirmations as coincidence or products of my imagination. I had been tied to the natural self for so long that true spiritual experiences seemed foreign.

One such incident occurred in the thick of the battle. I wrote in my journal: "For the past few weeks I've been slipping back into that bottomless pit. I could feel the adversary's hot breath and hear that horrid gnashing of teeth. Yesterday I felt overwhelmed. I decided failure was just a matter of time and I couldn't handle failing again.

"I had to work far into the night, and I was exhausted. I felt completely hopeless, so I decided to pray. I was tired of asking for strength. I was tired of 'having faith.' I was tired of 'trusting God.' I was tired.

"Somehow, I mustered up a 'Heavenly Father, I need help or I'm not going to make it. I can't do this anymore. Amen.' I didn't think much of it, only that I was disappointed I couldn't utter some profound prayer that would bring down the powers of heaven. I needed that so desperately.

"I finished my work and went outside for some air. The whole world was asleep. There were clouds blowing across the sky, much closer than usual. And every chance the moon got, it would come blaring through.

"Suddenly the veil was lifted for a fraction of a second, if eternities can be measured in seconds, and I saw the moon as a heavenly creation. It represented a world like the one I could help create someday—with a husband, no less. I felt I could reach up and grab the moon and start molding it. I've never had the 'life beyond' seem so real. And so attainable. It was like Heavenly Father was saying, 'You really can do this someday. You will do this someday.'

"It only lasted for an instant. I kept staring at the moon, hoping it would happen again. But mortality returned as quickly as it left. This morning I burned the toast, spent an hour looking for my keys, and got a phone call from Tracy. So much for godhood."

I did not fall again after that experience. I had my doubts and was sorely tempted, but I never succumbed. I think part of me knew I really couldn't handle another failure. Heavenly Father must have known, too, because He stepped in so majestically and with such mercy. I had never really thought of Heavenly Father as being merciful until then. I had thought He was cold and demanding. I didn't trust Him. I didn't think He really answered prayers.

Perhaps God really did answer prayers. Maybe He was willing to help. Maybe He didn't consider me to be some "pervert" unworthy of His attention.

Gradually, over the months and the years, the spiritual feelings became more frequent and longer in duration. They started to "enlighten my understanding." and "to be delicious to me." (Alma 32:28.) As they began to satisfy me, I began to desire them more than homosexual relationships.

"For ye know that the word hath swelled your souls, and ye also know that it hath sprouteth up, that your understanding doth begin to be enlightened, and your mind doth begin to expand. O then, is not this real? I say unto you, Yea, because it is light . . . [and] after ye have tasted this light is your knowledge perfect? Behold I say unto you, Nay; neither must ye lay aside your faith, for ye have only exercised your faith to plant the seed that ye might try the experiment to know if the seed was good. And behold, as the tree beginneth to grow, ye will say: Let us nourish it with great care, that it may get root, that it may grow up, and bring forth fruit unto us." (Alma 32:34–37.)

Some people, once they've gained confidence they can stay out of homosexual relationships, decide that because they've gone to the trouble of caring for the seed and helping it sprout, they shouldn't have to "nourish the tree as it beginneth to grow, by faith with great diligence, and with patience." They grow weary of the work it has taken to get to that point and want to live a "normal" life, one in which they don't have to work so diligently all the time.

Every stage of this battle involves a great deal of work. And the work must continue, with patience. "But if ye neglect the tree, and take no thought for its nourishment, behold it will not get any root; and when the heat of the sun cometh and scorcheth it, because it hath no root it withers away, and ye pluck it up and cast it out." (Alma 32:38.) And end up back in homosexual relationships.

Temptations of whatever sort—"the heat of the sun"—will surely follow us all the days of our mortal lives. But as faith increases, temptations lose their power.

EXERCISING FAITH

The first principle of the gospel is "faith in the Lord Jesus Christ." (Article of Faith 4.) Faith does not mean faith in our own power but in Christ's. Many feel they cannot overcome same-sex attraction.

Without the Savior, it probably is impossible. We must have faith in Him and in His ability to free us from the bondage of sin, if we will do our part.

Mighty, life-altering faith begins as a belief that Jesus is the Christ and that He has ultimate power. Gradually and consistently, faith must then be exercised. It works on the same principle as other types of exercise, requiring dedicated effort over time.

It's like starting at the bottom of a well where it's empty and dark. At some point you notice a tiny bit of light up top—hope. You see a way of escape because of the light. So you jump as hard as you can to reach the light and get yourself out, but you fall miserably short. You have tried and failed, so you become convinced it can't be done.

But several things have happened as a result of your efforts. One is that your muscles (your faith) have been slightly exercised. Another is that while you were jumping up, the hole began to be filled through the grace of the Lord according to your works. When you landed, you were closer to the light. The light of Christ within you also grew. You became somewhat "lighter," and the pull of the earth began to lose its power.

The changes are imperceptible to your human senses. All you know is that it's dark and it's empty and it's a long way out and you've already failed. Looking again toward the tiny bit of light up top, instead of at the darkness and emptiness below, can bring hope and greater faith to keep trying.

Some people, if they aren't in too deep, might manage to get out on their first or second try. It took me several attempts. As long as a person makes wholehearted attempts, exercises faith, and is patient through trials, God will continue to reward those efforts.

PRAYER

Prayer is vital in strengthening faith. "Pray always, that you may come off conqueror; yea, that you may conquer Satan, and that you may escape the hands of the servants of Satan that do uphold his work." (D&C 10:5.)

Satan is very aware of the power of prayer, so he seeks to dissuade people from praying. "For the evil spirit teacheth not a man to pray, but teacheth him that he must not pray." (2 Nephi 32:8.) He influences people to believe that prayer is a waste of time because Heavenly Father doesn't immediately fix the problem.

Satan also tells people they are not worthy to pray, which is another lie. Elder Richard G. Scott says: "If your life is in disarray and you feel uncomfortable and unworthy to pray because you are not clean, don't worry. [Heavenly Father] already knows about all of that. He is waiting for you to kneel in humility and take the first few steps." ("True Friends That Lift," *Ensign,* Nov. 1988, p. 77.)

Humility is just as important as feeling worthy to pray. "Be thou humble; and the Lord thy God shall lead thee by the hand, and give thee answer to thy prayers." (D&C 112:10.) To be humble, we must hand our will over to Heavenly Father.

SCRIPTURE STUDY

Satan tried to stop me from reading the scriptures and from believing that Christ's words applied to me. Despite his efforts, I gained a fervent testimony of scripture study. I would often read 1 Nephi 15:23–24 before reading other scriptures. "And they said unto me: What meaneth the rod of iron which our father saw, that led to the tree? And I said unto them that it was the word of God; and whoso would hearken unto the word of God, and would hold fast unto it, they would never perish; neither could the temptations and the fiery darts of the adversary overpower them unto blindness, to lead them away to destruction."

Consistent study of the scriptures provided more and more nourishment. I started to turn away from Satan's counterfeits and learned to "feast upon the words of Christ." (2 Nephi 32:3.)

THE LAW OF SACRIFICE

Another method of strengthening faith, or gaining more power, is sacrifice. To become like Christ, we must live the law of sacrifice in similitude of His great sacrifice. "I beseech you therefore, brethren, by the mercies of God, that ye present your bodies a living sacrifice, holy, acceptable unto God, which is your reasonable service. And be not conformed to this world: but be ye transformed by the renewing of your mind, that ye may prove what is that good, and acceptable, and perfect, will of God." (Romans 12:1–2.)

We are not to become conformed to homosexual desires; rather, we are to become transformed to the image of Christ. We must sacrifice homosexual relationships if we are to present our bodies holy unto God.

Blood sacrifice was done away with when Christ fulfilled the law, offering Himself as a sacrifice. Since that time, the requirement has been to "offer for a sacrifice unto me a broken heart and a contrite spirit." (3 Nephi 9:20.) A broken heart is one that desires the will of the Lord.

Power comes through sacrifice

To someone fighting against same-sex attraction, giving up homosexual relationships is a sacrifice of immense proportions. Heavenly Father and Jesus Christ are very aware of that. They know of the great pain and sacrifice involved. It is important to realize such sacrifices are recognized by heaven, even if they are not always acknowledged by those around us. One person wrote, "The sacrifice of a loved one for an attempt to live righteously cannot go unnoticed or unsupported. The loss is real. The sadness is real. The emptiness is real. The attempt is real. In a world where so few things are real, those things are real under any circumstance."

Satan is always right there, working both sides of the street. He, like the dishonest politician, stands ready to flip his story in an instant if it will serve his purposes. On the one hand he tried to convince me homosexual behavior was OK and I didn't have to give it up. Whenever I managed to make the sacrifice despite his efforts, he'd jump on the other side and say, "Oh, you disgusting sinner. That was no sacrifice. You shouldn't have been doing that nasty stuff in the first place. Maybe, if you're lucky and you're willing to suffer your whole life, you might catch up with the lowest of Saints." The adversary tries to convince people there is no sacrifice involved because he's very aware of the power that issues forth from such mighty acts of faith.

"Let us here observe, that a religion that does not require the sacrifice of all things never has power sufficient to produce the faith necessary unto life and salvation. . . .

"All the saints of whom we have account, in all the revelations of God which are extant, obtained the knowledge which they had of their acceptance in his sight through the sacrifice which they offered unto him; and through the knowledge thus obtained their faith became sufficiently strong to lay hold upon the promise of eternal life, and to endure as seeing him who is invisible; and were enabled, through faith, to combat the powers of darkness, contend against the wiles of the adversary, overcome the world, and obtain the end of their faith, even the salvation of their souls." (Joseph Smith, *Lectures on Faith,* 6:7, 11.)

Sacrifice allows us to "lay hold upon the promise of eternal life." It gives us the power to "contend against the wiles of the adversary [and] overcome the world." Through sacrifice, the struggle certainly becomes easier.

The voluntary offering of that which we value most

Sacrifices must be offered willingly, for that is what makes them sacrifices. We *give* them up. Heavenly Father will not take them against our will. The Roman soldiers did not take Christ's life. He freely gave it. "No man taketh it from me, but I lay it down of myself. I have power to lay it down, and I have power to take it again. This commandment have I received of my Father." (John 10:18.)

I don't know how many times I asked God to take away my homosexual desires when, in reality, I wasn't truly willing to give them up. Deep inside I still desired homosexual relationships more than doing God's will. I asked with my lips that He take them but held on tightly with my heart. "They draw near to me with their lips, but their hearts are far from me." (Joseph Smith–History 1:19.)

In time, He helped me loosen my grip. Still, I had to do much of the loosening myself. His desires gradually became my desires. I remained persistent, even when I was tempted to say, "Okay, Heavenly Father, I'll try it your way for a while. But then, if I'm not happy . . ."

Heavenly Father did not place us on this earth to test Him. He put us here to test us. And our test is to put Him above all else.

As the father of King Lamoni said before he underwent the mighty change of heart, "Yea, what shall I do that I may be born of God, having this wicked spirit rooted out of my breast, and receive his Spirit, that I may be filled with joy, that I may not be cast off at the last day? Behold, said he, I will give up all that I possess, yea, I will forsake my kingdom, that I may receive this great joy. . . . *I will give away all my sins to know thee.*" (Alma 22:15, 18; emphasis added.)

To be considered a sacrifice, something of value must be given up. We may find ourselves willing to sacrifice everything except what we value most, which is often what Heavenly Father wants us to give up. It's like giving a load of old clothes to Deseret Industries. We don't even consider giving away something nice. We go immediately to the old and tattered or the not-so-worn but out-of-style. Then we shove everything in a box and haul it off. Or better yet, we have them come and pick it up. And, as the D.I. truck drives away with the junk that was cluttering up our closets, we find ourselves thinking, "What a huge sacrifice I have just made."

We can't give up the things we don't care all that much about and keep the things that seem most precious but then claim to be living the law of sacrifice. It is a law fundamental to becoming like Christ. Our sacrifice must be in similitude of His. Obeying every other commandment and giving up everything else cannot compensate.

"Thou knowest the commandments, Do not commit adultery, Do not kill, Do not steal, Do not bear false witness, Defraud not, Honour thy father and mother. And [a certain ruler] said unto him, Master, all these have I observed from my youth. Then Jesus beholding him loved him, said unto him, one thing thou lackest: go thy way, sell whatsoever thou hast, and give to the poor, and thou shalt have treasure in heaven: and come, take up the cross, and follow me." (Mark 10:19–21.)

Jesus asked the man to give up that which he treasured most, and the man was very sorrowful because he felt he could not comply. Then Jesus observed, "How hard is it for them that trust in riches to enter into the kingdom of God!" (Mark 10:24.) This statement also refers to people who treasure anything more than the kingdom of God.

Abraham offered his son as a sacrifice, signifying to those of us who hope to be counted among the faithful that we must be willing to sacrifice whatever Heavenly Father requires. His requirements might be great.

Heavenly Father asks us to put upon the altar inappropriate relationships with people whom we may love deeply. In many ways that request does not make sense. Our understanding is limited. The natural heart and mind ask, "Why would God ask me to give up a relationship that means more to me than anything else?"

"And after many days an angel of the Lord appeared unto Adam, saying: Why dost thou offer sacrifices unto the Lord? And Adam said unto him: I know not, save the Lord commanded me." (Moses 5:6.) Giving up homosexual relationships has been the greatest sacrifice of my life. I did not understand the reasons at first, but even though "I knew not," I made the sacrifice because "the Lord commanded me."

Bearing up the cross

We must be willing to sacrifice all. Christ asks those who live a homosexual life to give up that life and bear up their cross. "If any man will come after me, let him deny himself, and take up his cross daily, and follow me. For whosoever will save his life shall lose it: but whosoever will lose his life for my sake, the same shall save it." (Luke 9:23–24.)

Joseph Smith's translation of this passage continues: "And now for a man to take up his cross, is to deny himself all ungodliness, and every worldly lust, and keep my commandments. Break not my commandments for to save your lives; for whosoever will save his life in this world, shall lose it in the world to come." (JST, Matthew 16:25–27.)

Most of the trials and suffering we are asked to endure in this life cannot be avoided once they have occurred—death of loved ones, abandonment, physical handicaps, accidents, or ill health. When God asks people to abandon homosexual relationships, they are sorely tempted to find an immediate means of escape from the resultant suffering by returning to those relationships.

Christ could have ended His hunger instantly by turning the stones into bread. He could have released Himself from the pain of the cross by letting Himself down. But He knew He had His cross to bear. *The* cross to bear. Even though the people shouted, "If thou be the Son of God, come down from the cross." (Matthew 27:40.) He knew that doing so would defeat the very purpose for which He had come into mortality. The Son of God proved His divinity as He bore His cross and fulfilled His mission.

Satan and others will shout, "Quit your suffering and come down from your cross. Prove who you really are: a homosexual." Christ says, "Take up your cross and follow Me. You are a child of God."

FAITH PRECEDES THE MIRACLE

Some say it would take a miracle to overcome homosexual behavior and desires. I disagree. In most cases, it will take several miracles.

"Have miracles ceased because Christ hath ascended into heaven, . . . Nay; neither have angels ceased to minister unto the children of men. . . . For it is by faith that miracles are wrought; and it is by faith that angels appear and minister unto men." (Moroni 7:27, 29, 37.)

Miracles are as real today as they were in times of old. I am certain of that, because I have witnessed them in my own life and in the lives of others. There is no earthly explanation for what I have seen take place.

Science can speculate about the causes and effects of homosexual desires and the impossibility of heterosexual desires emerging in such cases, but studying the world through natural minds can only bring a knowledge of the world as it appears. The grander reality is "Through faith we understand that the worlds were framed by the word of God, so that things which are seen were not made of things which do appear." (Hebrews 11:3.)

All of the scientific studies will never bring a complete understanding of things as they truly are. The mysteries of God will always remain mysteries to the natural, human mind. Faith exists in a dimension that includes science but extends far, far beyond it. Faith, not science, is the governing principle by which this world operates.

"Faith, then, is the first great governing principle which has power, dominion, and authority over all things; by it they exist, by it they are upheld, by it they are changed, or by it they remain, agreeable to the will of God." (*Lectures on Faith,* 1:24.)

The rewards of patience through trials of faith are great. We can drink from the "well of water springing up unto everlasting life." We can partake of the fruit of the "tree springing up unto everlasting life"—grown from a seed of hope to overcome—and not know hunger again.

Alma concludes his description of how to acquire and maintain faith: "And because of your diligence and your faith and your patience with the word in nourishing it, that it may take root in you, behold, by and by ye shall pluck the fruit thereof, which is most precious, which is sweet above all that is sweet, and which is white above all that is white, yea, and pure above all that is pure; and ye shall feast upon this fruit even until ye are filled, that ye hunger not, neither shall ye thirst." (Alma 32:42.)

CHAPTER 7

CHARITY—
The Pure Love of Christ

B ehold, I will show unto the Gentiles their weakness, and I will
show unto them that faith, hope and charity bringeth unto
me—the fountain of all righteousness." (Ether 12:28.) For "charity
is the pure love of Christ." (Moroni 7:47.)

I was once told, "The more we understand the gospel, the more
we understand love. The gospel is love."

All I knew about love ten years ago was that the love I felt in a
homosexual relationship far surpassed any other love I had ever
known. All I knew about the gospel was that it harshly commanded me to do the impossible—to give up love for something that felt
bitter and cold, condemning and calloused.

How could the gospel be love? It seemed to be just the opposite.
I had found what felt like true love, and the gospel required that I
give it up.

"You can't have it!"

The gospel wanted me to sacrifice the very thing that had come
to mean everything to me. I had finally found a place where I
belonged. I'd found warmth and acceptance and a caring touch. The
pain was finally gone.

"Can't you understand? The pain is finally gone!"

I felt that the gospel expected me to endure the pains of hell my
entire life so maybe I could reach the celestial kingdom in some distant lifetime.

"How can the gospel be love?"

"For unto you is born this day in the city of David, a Saviour, which is Christ the Lord. And this shall be a sign unto you; Ye shall find the babe wrapped in swaddling clothes, lying in a manger."

"And they clothed him with purple, and platted a crown of thorns, and put it about his head, and began to salute him, Hail, King of the Jews! And they smote him on the head with a reed, and did spit upon him, and bowing their knees worshipped him. And when they had mocked him, they took off the purple from him, and put his own clothes on him, and led him out to crucify him." (Luke 2:11–12; Mark 15:17–20.)

For "behold the sufferings and death of him who did no sin." (D&C 45:4.) Innocent as a newborn, He was rejected, mocked, and crucified. Any apparent unfairness in this world is swallowed up in the life and death and resurrection of Jesus Christ.

And love? "Greater love hath no man than this, that a man lay down his life for his friends." (John 15:13.)

For unto each one of us, personally, was born that day in the city of David our Savior, who is Christ, the Lord. And for each and every one of us He suffered pains and afflictions and temptations throughout His life so "that he may know according to the flesh how to succor his people according to their infirmities." (Alma 7:12.) He bled from every pore at Gethsemane and suffered upon the cross for us.

That is the gospel of Jesus Christ, and Jesus Christ is love. The gospel *is* love—true, undefiled love, which is called charity.

Christ has gone forth as our Examplar. If we choose to follow Him, we will surely have to suffer also, even innocently at times. The sacrifices that will be required may even include our relationships with those we love.

Heavenly Father sacrificed His Son, whom He loved perfectly, showing that He loves each of us perfectly. "For God so loved the world, that he gave his only begotten Son, that whosoever believeth in him should not perish, but have everlasting life. For God sent not his Son into the world to condemn the world; but that the world through him might be saved." (John 3:16–17.)

I used to think God was condemning me, not trying to save me. I refused to believe that God is love. I was convinced the whole challenge of same-sex attraction was a big, horrible joke. I felt as though we were all pawns in the chess game of life and the gods sat up there laughing each time they flicked an unsuspecting pawn off the edge of the universe.

Eventually I came to realize that Heavenly Father's plan of salvation is my plan of salvation, too. And not only has the plan been designed to save me but it also has been designed to bring me joy, peace, and love beyond measure—here on earth as well as throughout all eternity.

I used to think I was doing Heavenly Father and Jesus Christ a monumental favor by leaving homosexual relationships. Now I understand that they asked me to overcome sin because of their great love for me and because they want me eventually to become as they are and share in all that they have. I now realize I did *myself* a monumental favor by abandoning homosexual relationships.

LOVE THYSELF AS THY NEIGHBOR

Heavenly Father and Christ love all of mankind. We are to follow their examples by loving and accepting ourselves as well as others. I wish I could have been as loving and generous toward myself as I was with other people. Instead, I hated myself. I did not comprehend the meaning of the scripture "love thy neighbor as thyself."

True, this scripture asks us to love our neighbor, but it also asks us to love ourselves. For some, it might help to switch the order of the comparison—"love thyself as thy neighbor." People often have just as much difficulty, if not more, following the admonition to love self.

Satan is quite accustomed to hatred. Coaxing us to hate ourselves is his area of expertise. "You're unworthy. You'll never change. You'll never be anything but bad." I began hating myself after the sexual molestations. The hatred intensified along with my same-sex attraction, alcohol abuse, and many unsuccessful attempts to overcome both.

Whether a person is involved in homosexual behavior every single day or struggling with leftover feelings on occasion, the worth of that soul is great in the sight of the Lord. He loves each one of us, individually, and wants to help us return to Him. He talks of the value of the lost coin and the lost sheep.

We are told of a father—likened unto our Heavenly Father—who rejoiced the moment his prodigal son returned home: "But when he was yet a great way off, his father saw him, and had compassion, and ran, and fell on his neck, and kissed him." (Luke 15:20.) The immediate warm reception offered by the father indicates he was not angry and ashamed, suddenly changing his feelings the moment his son returned. He had love for his son all along, even when he "wasted his substance with riotous living." (Luke 15:13.)

Christ loves the sinner at every point of progression, as should we. He performed the ultimate act to prove that for "while we were yet sinners, Christ died for us." (Romans 5:8.)

COMFORT THROUGH THE LOVE OF CHRIST

Jesus Christ seeks to comfort us and show us His love. Before this earth life we walked with Him and talked with Him. Now a thick veil stands in the way. It is difficult to reach to hands that eyes cannot see and listen to voices that ears cannot hear. It can seem an unbearable challenge to stop seeking wholeness and comfort from homosexual relationships, enduring the pain and loneliness of spiritual stretching until Christ's love can be felt as He encircles each one of us "in the arms of [His] love." (D&C 6:20.)

Amazingly, the person who teaches us the most about charity is Moroni. He wandered alone for years after his family and loved ones had been killed. He was surrounded by war and bloodshed. Yet there, all alone in the midst of the upheaval, he spoke not of his plight or unbearable loneliness; rather, he powerfully testified of his father's words concerning charity. Moroni had something to "cleave unto." He was upheld and comforted by the pure love of Christ: "Wherefore, my beloved brethren, if ye have not charity, ye are nothing, for charity never faileth. Wherefore, cleave unto charity, which is the greatest of all." (Moroni 7:46.)

Some people struggling with same-sex attraction fear they will have to spend the rest of their lives alone, without a close relationship with someone. But what "alone" feels like in the midst of the struggle is not what it feels like later. The love of Christ at first may seem little more than emptiness, but that's because sin or confusion or resentment or guilt or false feelings of unworthiness or all of those things stand in the way.

I used to think homosexual relationships brought pure love. Now I realize that pure love is not obtained by pursuing passions. It is gained by keeping passions within the guidelines set by the Lord. As Alma said, "Bridle all your passions, that ye may be filled with love"—the pure love of Christ. (Alma 38:12.)

I am not alone. I now have a close, personal relationship with the Lord Jesus Christ. And I prefer a close relationship with the Savior over a homosexual relationship. It is impossible to maintain both. As Elder Neal A. Maxwell has said, "Whatever we embrace instead of Christ will keep us from being embraced by Him!" (Address given to Church Educational System area directors, Salt Lake City, 1 Oct. 1992.)

I bear testimony that Christ's redeeming love truly is redeeming. Several months ago I became discouraged and overwhelmed. I reread my life story for the umpteenth time and came to the poem I had written:

> Dear God, it's black again.
> Two solid months of darkness.
> Two solid days of light marked Christ's arrival.
>
> I guess He isn't coming.
>
> Have faith, you say?
> But faith does not hold my hand.
> Or stroke my hair and tell me I'm OK.

I did not get any further than that. Something, or someone, stroked my hair. I was overcome with the Spirit, physically as well as spiritually. I realized in a powerful, new way that I was okay, that the Savior was there for me. I wish I could express how real it was—somehow convey in words the incredible feeling of peace and comfort and love undefiled.

I know that Christ lives and that He is with me. And because of that, nothing else really matters. My family and close friends could be taken away. My home could be destroyed. I could go bankrupt. My health could deteriorate. And even though those trials would be extremely difficult, life couldn't be as difficult as it had been without the constant companionship of the Lord's Spirit.

The empty places in my life are now filled with love. I have an enduring sense of fulfillment. Human relationships can falter, but "charity never faileth."

CHAPTER 8

REPENTANCE—
Putting Off the Natural Self

R epentance. The Greek word of which this is the translation denotes a change of mind, i.e., a fresh view about God, about oneself, and about the world. Since we are born into conditions of mortality, repentance comes to mean a turning of the heart and will to God, and a renunciation of sin to which we are naturally inclined." ("Repentance," LDS Bible Dictionary, p. 760.)

I used to view repentance as punishment, as something I had to do because I had been bad. In actuality, repentance is a process of growth and change. As our will is turned toward God, we become aligned with Him and His commandments. Then the powers of heaven can flow freely. Repentance brings freedom from the natural self, allowing the body to conform to the true self.

Repentance includes more than cleansing from sin. Not only does Christ pay the price for our sins and help us to remove them from our lives but He also takes "the pains and the sicknesses of his people." (Alma 7:11.) That is especially important with regard to same-sex attraction. Some people struggle with homosexual desires yet have never acted on them. They've done all they can to rid themselves of the desires but without success. Through the redeeming process of repentance, a person can put off the natural self and its homosexual desires, whether or not those desires have been acted upon.

As much as we would like growth to take place instantly, the Alcoholics Anonymous motto of "one day at a time" applies. The process of gaining freedom takes time, effort, and patience. But we are human and therefore impatient by nature. We came to earth from a place that had no clocks. No second hands. No calendars by which to mark off day after painstaking day of personal progress. Or personal defeat.

The process of finding freedom from same-sex attraction is often slow and very involved. For example, in this chapter I discuss nearly two hundred actions a person can take to help put off the natural self. I learned to avoid becoming disheartened when there seemed to be so much more I should have been doing. It was impossible to work on more than a few things at a time.

Enduring a day without sexual contact can mark great success if a person has previously been unable to do so. When Satan fails to stop us from trying to overcome, he seeks to convince us that we can't try hard enough and might as well give up.

My process involved several years of effort, during which I was strengthened and found increased freedom all along the way. I used to become anxious, losing sight of the necessity to concentrate on doing what I could. I'd pray: "OK, Heavenly Father, tonight I promise that I will never again be sexually involved with a woman. I'll never think about it again. I'll never go to another bar. I'll find new friends. I'll go to church every Sunday. I'll quit drinking and doing drugs. I'll quit smoking. I'll read my scriptures every day. I'll complete a service project at least once a month. . . . Oh yeah, and I'll keep praying every night and every morning and at least once in the middle of the day. I promise these things from this night forward. Amen." By the following Monday I'd usually have managed to break every single promise. I finally learned to do what I could and be grateful for whatever progress was made.

I have gained a greater understanding of the entire process of repentance. After a friend pointed out that repentance applies not only to sin but to all parts of the natural self, I came to understand how it applied to me and my struggle. Looking back, I can see in my process of coming unto Christ the seven aspects of repentance:

recognition, sorrow, confession, forsaking, restitution, forgiveness, and keeping the commandments.

Several of the aspects of repentance occurred simultaneously and in no particular order. They are not separate, ordered stages. Various parts of each aspect occurred over a period of several years.

RECOGNITION

First I had to recognize that homosexual behavior and the fostering of lustful feelings are sin. Because "if we say that we have no sin, we deceive ourselves, and the truth is not in us." (1 John 1:8.) I began to heed the scripture, "Let your sins trouble you, with that trouble which shall bring you down unto repentance. O my son, I desire that ye should deny the justice of God no more. Do not endeavor to excuse yourself in the least point because of your sins, by denying the justice of God; but do you let the justice of God, and his mercy, and his long-suffering have full sway in your heart." (Alma 42:29–30.)

Recognition of the true self vs. the natural self

People who are trapped in homosexual behavior sometimes believe that their false self is the person who goes to church and pretends to be a happy heterosexual. They feel they have to hide the self they believe to be their true self—their homosexual self—in order to find acceptance. In reality, the true self desires to go to church because it recalls and recognizes the truthfulness of the gospel. Part of the true self feels ill at ease in church because love and acceptance are important spiritual needs. Love that might be felt from the true Christians at church is blocked because of the fear of rejection.

Heavenly Father does not ask us to become someone we're not, although that may seem to be so in the case of homosexual attractions. He asks us to put off the natural self and become who we truly are. Our eternal identity, or true self, "contributes to our earthly personality and is influenced by earthly experiences. It is also the enduring, fundamental self that can transcend circumstance, culture, race, genetics, or other temporal and temporary influences. It is the internal essence of what we are and of what we may become."

(Richard L. Bednar and Scott R. Peterson, *Spirituality and Self-Esteem* [Salt Lake City: Deseret Book Co., 1990], p. 16.)

The natural self, along with the God-given sexual desires that have been misdirected, creates the sexual part of same-sex attraction. It is the natural self, not the true self, that desires to go against the word of God.

The true self seeks a sense of belonging, unconditional love, safety, fulfillment, and intimacy. Heavenly Father does not intend for us to be deprived of the fulfillment of legitimate needs. He asks us to find ways of meeting them within the boundaries He has set.

Acceptance is an extremely important and legitimate need. Self-acceptance is especially significant, which is probably why Satan seeks to warp our perception of it. He would have us accept our sins.

Bruce C. Hafen states that "if you are made uncomfortable by restraining your sexual urges, then (the reasoning goes) accept the liberation of just being honest about yourself. Accept yourself for what you are. It's unnatural to try to be someone you're not." He points out that the current trend in popular psychology is to use self-acceptance as the goal rather than the starting point. (*The Broken Heart* [Salt Lake City: Deseret Book Co., 1989], pp. 180–81.)

Self-acceptance—realizing trials that need to be overcome and loving yourself in spite of them—is just the beginning. Behavior must still be overcome. Yet self-acceptance is the critical starting point. Few people choose the trial of same-sex attraction. No one is inherently bad or evil because of it.

When I thought my homosexual desires were part of my true self, I tried to keep my true self hidden for fear of being rejected or hurt. Unfortunately, that kept my emotions and many aspects of my personality hidden also. Slowly, I let my true self come out. I admitted to having homosexual desires, yet I began to separate myself from them and accept myself.

Recognition of what has contributed to same-sex attraction

Most of my recognition came in the confession stage when I discussed past difficulties with my bishop, counselor, and others who had the Spirit and the power of discernment. One thing that at first hindered me from going through the recognition process was the fear that if I did find events and circumstances that contributed to my feelings, then I couldn't say, "It's just the way I am." A lack of apparent causes did not excuse my homosexual behavior. Denying problems only made it more difficult to repent

Seemingly trivial events often contribute to same-sex attraction. One woman who struggles with homosexual feelings remembered having a very close friend in the third grade. The two were inseparable, which is common at that age. They sat next to each other until the day the teacher decided to arrange the class in alphabetical order. When the girls put up a fuss, the teacher sharply commented that it was odd they were so close. It seemed like a small matter, but it put the idea in her head that there was something wrong with her and with her feelings toward the other girl.

I began to uncover events from my past that kept me attached to my natural self. I also looked for things that made it more difficult to obey any of God's commandments. I realized that several of my problems were a result of my homosexual attractions rather than a cause of them. Because of the conflict, my relationship with Heavenly Father, Christ, and His restored gospel were severely damaged.

SORROW

"Godly sorrow worketh repentance." (2 Corinthians 7:10.) It was difficult for me to feel sorrow for homosexual relationships because they often did not feel wrong.

One evening, long after I had agreed to stop seeing Tracy, I went in to talk with my bishop. He had been very supportive and understanding for many, many months while I grieved deeply over the loss of my relationship with Tracy. That night the Spirit apparently knew it was time for me to stop mourning and get on with my life. I was told there was a scripture I needed to hear and study. Feeling sorry for myself, I expected "thine adversity and thine afflictions shall be but a small moment" (D&C 121:7) or "blessed are all they that mourn, for they shall be comforted." (3 Nephi 12:4.)

Instead, the bishop proclaimed, "But behold this my joy was vain, for their sorrowing was not unto repentance, because of the goodness of God; but it was rather the sorrowing of the damned, because the Lord would not always suffer them to take happiness in sin." (Mormon 2:13.)

Ouch.

Although sorrowing for the loss of Tracy was important, it came to have a negative effect. The sorrow brought regret for having left the relationship, and I longed to return to it. The time had finally arrived for me to stop feeling sorry for myself and start feeling sorry for the sins I had committed. Godly sorrow for sin took the need for change to a feeling level. Christ's life became real and present. I sensed that it was only the human part of Christ that had suffered in the Garden and on the cross two thousand years ago. The part of Him that was God transcended time to bring together all the suffering of every human being who had lived or would live on this earth. He went to each of our moments of suffering in each of our lives to encompass it all. I felt that His great suffering in the Garden and on the cross was taking place now, today.

I sorrowed for the sins I had committed, for causing Christ to suffer innocently on my behalf. Godly sorrow brought with it a gratitude so deep I was propelled toward further righteousness in an attempt to pay back, in some small way, the debt I owed.

CONFESSION

I sat in a strange congregation in a new building. After months of wavering, I had finally decided to find my ward and my bishop in order to confess. As if it weren't frightening and humiliating enough to tell a total stranger about my private life, I had to tell him about my homosexual activity.

I felt angry, ashamed, humiliated, and paralyzed with fear. It was a miracle that I sat through sacrament meeting, fought the crowds up to the front, pulled that strange man by the sleeve, and asked to speak with him in private.

That strange man helped change my life. I'd made the mistake of thinking confession was used to issue strong judgments against people. For the serious sins, confession is used, in part, to determine if people are worthy to retain their Church memberships. But it is so much more than that. "He that covereth his sins shall not prosper:

but whoso confesseth and forsaketh them shall have mercy." (Proverbs 28:13.)

To keep sin and weakness hidden means to keep sin and weakness. Sinful desires tend to feed on themselves. Thinking evil thoughts took me further from God's thinking and closer to Satan's. Confession helped pierce the darkness and break through the cloud cover. When I expressed my feelings, the bishop could shed light—eternal light—on my life. Opening up allowed the Spirit of truth to come in.

Satan tries to convince us we can go it alone because he knows we can't. A wise, all-knowing Heavenly Father has required confession to the proper authority so healing can occur.

The power of the priesthood

My bishop helped me not only because he was a judge in Israel who determined whether I could keep my Church membership, but because he represented God and guided me with the power of the holy priesthood. He offered helpful advice not because he had handled the issue of same-sex attraction before, but because he was in tune with the Spirit.

Some individuals have not had as positive an experience with their Church leaders as I did with mine. I have friends who live a homosexual life and refuse ever to confess again because their experiences with their bishops were negative, even degrading. We need to work together to increase understanding.

Others, who have had difficulty with their bishop, have sought assistance from their stake president. It's important to develop a relationship with someone who can exercise righteous priesthood stewardship.

I sometimes had difficulties with "the priesthood" and "men in power" until I came to understand that the priesthood is not the power of man but the power of God. Its power blesses everyone who lives worthy of it. Men hold the administrative keys, but all enjoy its power. Even though the priesthood may be abused and mishandled on occasion, and some priesthood leaders have made mistakes while exercising their stewardship, Heavenly Father's plan can and does prevail. It is perfect. Humans are not.

Heaven can provide perfect strength and perfect love. Prayers for a priesthood leader to be inspired to give proper guidance can help. Priesthood blessings can loosen the grip of the natural self. The power of God manifest through the priesthood is greater than any homosexual desire.

Professional counseling

Opening up to a counselor accelerated my healing process. I strongly encourage professional counseling for anyone struggling to gain freedom from same-sex attraction. But carefully research and pray when selecting a counselor. Most counselors outside of the Church—and even some within—believe that the goal of counseling should be to help clients with homosexual desires learn to accept and act on those desires.

Emotional upheaval is often created while working through homosexual behavior, desires, and conflicts. The process can be long and involved. Still, it is important to express feelings and emotions in a setting where experienced, professional feedback can be given, without biases being shared. Both counselors I chose were LDS. Their belief in me and my ability to overcome helped increase my belief in myself. The presence of the Spirit was a mighty facilitator throughout the process. Having counselors who were guided spiritually as well as professionally helped me a great deal.

Opening up to others

Researchers Martha and John Beck found that compulsive behaviors occur in a cycle of four stages. The first stage is feelings of isolation, which lead to the second stage—actions of self-indulgence. Self-indulgence leads to feelings of self-hatred, which then lead to actions of self-concealment. The concealment leads to more feelings of isolation, and the cycle continues. Rather than concealing their struggle, individuals who have determined to leave homosex-ual relationships can share their burdens with other true followers of Christ to begin breaking the cycle by dissipating feelings of isolation. (See Breaking the Cycle of Compulsive Behavior [Salt Lake City: Deseret Book Co., 1990], pp. 17, 70, 96.)

The fear of telling anyone "straight" makes breaking free from homosexual behavior and desires very difficult. Most of the people I talked with openly were "living the lifestyle." I finally learned to counsel with those who were devoted to the fulness of the gospel.

Releasing emotions

Not only was confession important in helping with my feelings of isolation but it also helped release the hold that past experiences and the feelings attached to those experiences had on my life. After I abandoned homosexual relationships and drug use, I experienced a barrage of feelings and needs those behaviors had been temporarily satisfying or covering up.

"People who are addicted look for something to rely upon. And one thing about drugs, sex, food and excitement, they always do what they promise [for a time]. You can depend upon them. With them you learn to feel okay and competent. But then without them, you'll feel empty and defeated." (Patrick Carnes, *Don't Call It Love* [New York: Bantam Books, 1991], p. 94.)

Homosexual relationships, alcohol, and drugs had previously masked many of my feelings. I also used compulsive work habits to avoid dealing with issues I really needed to face. Without them I felt not only empty and defeated but also desperate, panicked, lonely, and depressed. For a while, all I could do was hold my own. The longer I obeyed the Word of Wisdom and other laws of the gospel, the more able I became to unload layer after layer of feelings and emotions and the more the Spirit was able to assist. Emotions were identified, examined, felt, and released.

The strongest, most binding emotions were anger, guilt, shame, fear, and sadness. I learned that emotions needed to be examined and expressed *before* forgiving. Forced forgiveness blocks access to unreleased feelings. For instance, anger is often directed inward and can cause severe depression and result in addictive behaviors. It is also directed at such innocent bystanders as Heavenly Father, friends, or the guy in the car just ahead who changed lanes a little too quickly.

It is not always possible or appropriate to express grief and anger directly to those who have inflicted it. Still, it is important to express those feelings. Writing a letter that's never sent or working through feelings with a counselor or friend can help. Only after feelings are expressed can true forgiveness come.

I had difficulty releasing anger. After all, "true Christians don't get angry." But I learned that just as Christ became angry at the money changers who defiled the temple of God, I had every right to express anger when my body and mind—my temple of God—had been defiled. It was righteous indignation on behalf of myself as an innocent child.

In addition to anger, I uncovered intense sadness over the loss of my childhood. I discovered I had never really mourned that loss. Many of the emotions I had felt as a child—reactions to trauma—had not been expressed because I hadn't been able to handle them at the time of the experiences.

Children can develop amazing defense systems that help them survive trauma. Unfortunately, they often continue to use those same defenses when they become adults. What they needed to shut down on at one point needs to be expressed appropriately later. Those feelings, left unexpressed, can keep people tied to other negative feelings or destructive habits that were used as protection against the pain.

Overcoming resentment toward Heavenly Father

When emotions such as those resulting from abuse were finally brought out to be worked through, it was like stirring up murky waters after the junk had previously settled to the bottom. My soul became cloudy, and it was difficult to feel and see the light of the Spirit through the debris. I would feel abandoned and resentful. Gradually, however, I learned to have faith that although I could not always sense their presence, Heavenly Father and Christ were always there for me.

Part of my anger toward Heavenly Father was a result of my fear of Him. I thought He was lying in wait to punish me, and my anger served to keep me at a safe distance. I was also angry with God because I thought my struggle with same-sex attraction was imposed by Him, rather than by Satan.

Some people have difficulties in their relationship with Heavenly Father because they project their feelings toward men or their own father onto Him. My relationship with Heavenly Father was damaged by the sexual abuse I suffered.

As I worked through the effects of the abuse, I uncovered my resentment toward Heavenly Father. One night I was praying that Heavenly Father's and Christ's "maleness" would cease to interfere with my receptiveness to the Spirit. Somewhere in the middle of it all I heard myself say, "I know that thou art not man. Thou art God. And Jesus is the Christ." The power of those words transformed my feelings toward Heavenly Father and Jesus Christ.

"As man is, God once was." God once was human, but He is now a perfected Being who loves us perfectly in a way that is difficult for us, as mortals, to comprehend.

Moving on

I discovered that Christ was very willing and able to take up feelings once I had expressed them and given them to Him. Some experiences came up more than once. Years later I went back to events I thought I'd worked through, only to discover they'd been waiting for me to gain the spiritual and emotional strength I needed to work through the feelings at a deeper level.

Negative feelings—even those we think we are entitled to, such as anger, unforgiveness, and resentment—create areas of darkness within us that block the light of Christ. Eventually I was able to let go and move on, instead of carrying my past trials and resentments around as if they were medals I'd earned. It became time for me to stop seeking sympathy from myself, the Spirit, and others. There was a life with Christ that needed to be lived.

FORSAKING

I thought I had to forsake my sins before I could confess them. I don't know how many times I had said to myself, "Well, I'll see the bishop next month, after I've given up the relationship." But I could not find the power to overcome until I enlisted the help of others.

Forsaking is the part of repentance that involves the 180-degree turn, away from homosexuality and toward Christ. Once I started making the turn, Satan did all he could to stop me from completing it. He sought to cheat me by degrees. "Ah, this is no big deal. God

will justify a little sin. Don't worry about it; there is no harm in this.
Perhaps God will beat you with a few stripes, and at last you shall
be saved in the kingdom of God. Have no fear." (See 2 Nephi 28:8.)
I learned that I could not come unto Christ by consistently veering in
other directions. "Because strait is the gate, and narrow is the way."
(Matthew 7:14.)

Forsaking occurred at different stages, just as every other aspect
of repentance does. Initially, refraining from sexual encounters was
all I could do. I knew my actions had to be changed if my feelings
were to change. "Commit thy works unto the Lord, and thy thoughts
shall be established." (Proverbs 16:3.) In turn, as my thoughts and
feelings changed—becoming rooted and established in Christ—it
became progressively easier to change my behavior.

I had the most difficulty giving up my emotional dependency
on women. Although it was difficult and seemingly impossible at
times for me to avoid sexual involvement, I was most closely bound
by the emotional aspects of relationships with women.

It seems that women struggle with emotional dependency to a
greater degree than men, although both are susceptible. It is not
uncommon for a woman to overcome sexual behavior and remain
emotionally enmeshed in another woman's life. Sexual dependency
occurs more frequently with men. Of course, those are generalizations, and women as well as men may struggle with either dependency.

Both dependencies can also be found in heterosexual relationships and are just as spiritually corrosive. Although the following sec-
tions are directed to those with homosexual inclinations, some
points apply universally.

Forsaking emotional dependency

Emotional dependency is difficult because it is easiest to rationalize. "Well, we aren't sexually involved, so there is no sin. I just
want a 'soul mate.'" I rationalized my attachment to Tracy long after
we managed to avoid sexual contact. We still talked on the phone
quite often and visited on occasion. Fortunately we lived in different
states by the time I returned to church, but I continued to think
about her all the time.

I didn't understand that making another person the most important being in my life was a form of idolatry. "Thou shalt have no other gods before me." (Exodus 20:3.) Who did I worship? Who was the most important being in my life? Who did I always think about and talk to and seek to please? To whom did I offer my sacrifices? To whom did I give my heart? The answer was not God.

President Ezra Taft Benson has said, "When we put God first, all other things fall into their proper place or drop out of our lives. Our love of the Lord will govern the claims for our affection, the demands on our time, the interests we pursue, and the order of our priorities.

"We should put God ahead of *everyone else* in our lives." ("The Great Commandment—Love the Lord," *Ensign,* May 1988, p. 4; italics in original.)

The scriptures say, "Let all thy thoughts be directed unto the Lord; yea, let the affections of thy heart be placed upon the Lord forever." (Alma 37:36.) When I was honest, I had to admit that the affections of my heart were placed upon Tracy, not the Lord. But the more I looked to Christ and Christians for support, the more I was able to rely on the Savior.

"Emotional dependency is *the condition resulting when the ongoing presence and/or nurturing is believed necessary for personal security. . . .* Whether or not physical involvement exists, sin enters the picture when a friendship becomes a dependent relationship." The following is a partial list of the indicators of an emotionally dependent relationship.

"When either party in a relationship:
• experiences frequent jealousy, possessiveness and a desire for exclusivism, viewing other people as a threat to the relationship.
• prefers to spend time alone with this friend and becomes frustrated when this does not happen.
• loses interest in friendships other than this one.
• experiences romantic or sexual feelings leading to fantasy about this person.
• is unwilling to make short- or long-range plans that do not include the other person.
• displays physical affection beyond that which is appropriate for a friendship.

•refers frequently to the other in conversation; feels free to 'speak for' the other." (Lori Thorkelson Rentzel, *Emotional Dependency* [San Rafael, Calif.: Exodus International, 1984], pp. 1–4; itaics in original.)

It requires a great deal of honesty to determine whether you have become more dependent on someone else than on the Lord. Seek counsel from Heavenly Father and from those who have stewardship over you or from friends who are inspired (not, of course, the friend in question).

Dr. Carol Ahrens describes emotionally dependent relationships among women: "They call it a 'special friendship' (sometimes even believing that it's a godsend), one that is unlike any they've had before. They've finally met somebody who makes them feel wonderfully loved, totally satisfied. Other friendships pale in comparison, and soon all socializing centers around this one person, the great companion, this emotional idol. And, as idols do, this person begins to hold tremendous power."

Later she states, "If you are involved in an emotionally dependent relationship, you need to withdraw from it. . . . You'll be tempted to negotiate this decision by perhaps telling yourself you can keep seeing this person a little less often, call each other occasionally, and still remain friends. But experience has shown this to be impossible, because you're accustomed to very intense, intimate relating with your friend, and chances are you'll fall back into the old patterns if you give yourself a chance to. A clean break is necessary." (Quoted in Joe Dallas, *Desires in Conflict* [Eugene, Oreg.: Harvest House, 1991], pp. 207, 209–10.)

Emotional dependency without sexual involvement will rarely, if ever, bring Church membership into question. Nevertheless, sin is still involved. Such a relationship blocks the person from learning to depend upon the Lord and from developing attractions toward the opposite sex.

Forsaking sexual dependency

In discussing sexual dependency, I rely heavily upon my meetings with counselors who have specialized in same-sex attraction, books on the subject, and conversations with friends who are dealing with this issue in their own lives. I do not know what it feels like to be sexually dependent, but I do know what it's like to struggle with strong sexual temptation.

When trying to resist sexually acting out, it's important to concentrate not only on discontinuing the behavior but also on the feelings that are driving the behavior. Denying, suppressing, or ignoring those feelings can worsen the problem. If you've ever tried to defend homosexual behavior and said, "It's about more than just sex. It's about . . . " Finish the sentence, and then find ways to meet those needs within the Lord's boundaries. It might be about love, acceptance, self-worth, or comfort.

A trusted friend you can call whenever you feel the urge to act out can be a vital source of strength. Discuss what you're feeling and why. Ceasing to act out sexually can bring a deluge of emotions because homosexual relationships are often used as protection against such feelings. The emotions must be felt and released, not suppressed, in order for the drive toward sexual relationships to lose its power.

Dr. William Consiglio recommends learning your "setups" and avoiding them whenever possible. Setups are the people, events, or circumstances that provoke certain emotions, which in turn provoke acting out sexually. He identifies fifteen groups of emotions as triggers: feeling unloved and worthless, anxious and depressed, angry and irritated, ridiculed and humiliated, disregarded and ignored, violated and abused, guilty and shamed, incompetent and inadequate, fearful and frightened, rejected and condemned, failing and defeated, weak and lacking confidence, helpless and hopeless, victimized and oppressed, and, lastly, self-pitying, sad, and overwhelmed. I add lonely to the list (as if the list were not quite long enough already).

He explains that it is important to be proactive rather than continually feeling acted upon by circumstances and emotions. "Proacting means to make positive, constructive, and forceful responses to overcoming these protective reactions and coming to grips with your wounded emotions." (*Homosexual No More* [Wheaton, Ill.: Victor Books, 1991], p. 165.)

Stephen R. Covey lists being proactive as the first habit people should develop when seeking to make positive changes in their lives: "Look at the word *responsibility*—'response-ability'—the ability to choose your response. Highly proactive people recognize that responsibility. They do not blame circumstances, conditions, or conditioning for their behavior. Their behavior is a product of their own conscious choice, based on values, rather than a product of their conditions, based on feeling." (*The Seven Habits of Highly Effective People* [New York: Simon and Schuster, 1989], p. 71.)

Thinking you have no choice about becoming sexually involved diminishes your personal power. "Wherefore, men are free according to the flesh; and all things are given them which are expedient unto man. And they are free to choose liberty and eternal life, through the great Mediator of all men, or to choose captivity and death, according to the captivity and power of the devil; for he seeketh that all men might be miserable like unto himself." (2 Nephi 2:27.)

Individuals may have had little or no control over the factors that caused their first homosexual attractions, but at some point, they chose to continue thinking about those attractions and acting upon them. Believing that you never had any control over acting out can cause you to believe you do not have control over *refraining* from acting out.

Forsaking thoughts

Homosexual behaviors and desires cannot be overcome if those desires are continually fed. Pornography, fantasizing, and masturbation only fuel the fire. A seemingly accurate rationalization is, "Well, at least I'm not committing any great sin." Jesus counsels us, "And verily I say unto you, as I have said before, he that looketh on a woman to lust after her, or if any shall commit adultery in their hearts, they shall not have the Spirit, but shall deny the faith and shall fear." (D&C 63:16.) The Spirit is essential for gaining freedom, and lust forces the Spirit to leave, greatly diminishing needed faith.

Thinking of sin also affects the mind. In sports, the power of imagery is sometimes used. For instance, imagining making successful shots in basketball is a form of practicing. Confidence is improved because a person considers himself or herself to be a high-percentage shooter. The subconscious mind can't tell the difference between the imagined and the actual experience.

The same principle applies to overcoming homosexual behavior and the "gay identity." As a person holds to the thoughts and images of homosexual relationships, it becomes next to impossible to consider himself or herself to be anything other than a homosexual and to act like anything other than a homosexual.

I couldn't stop thinking certain thoughts unless I replaced them with something else. I used conscious, mental exertion to replace thoughts about sin with thoughts related to the Savior and other positive aspects of my life.

After I was able to forsake lustful thoughts, I began to forsake reminiscing. The thought beginning, "Gee, it was sure nice back then . . ." was potentially catastrophic. It could set in motion an avalanche of perilous thinking: "Yes, I remember when. . . . Oh, I do miss it. I want it. I need it! It's how I am! I can't change, and I never will! I am gay forever!"

It went something like that. I call it the Satan Snowball Effect, and I learned to take notice whenever a single flake fell.

Eventually forsaking included getting rid of old letters and photographs, discontinuing the seemingly innocent phone call or occasional visit, and avoiding places where I was likely to meet people looking for homosexual relationships. (I realize that can include even the grocery store, but I avoided the more obvious places.)

Dreams were frequently difficult for me. Years after leaving homosexual relationships, even after I had forsaken conscious homosexual thoughts, I'd have sexual dreams that would set me back. Dreams have a way of digging up feelings again. Looking back, I think sometimes the timing of the dreams helped me work through more emotions. Often the timing was lousy, and I'd slip back into the old "See, I haven't changed, and I never will" routine.

After enough setbacks I realized that dreams have about as much significance as we care to give them. I learned simply not to give them any heed. I forsook thinking about them.

Eventually, everything remotely attached to homosexual relationships has to be forsaken. To forsake does not mean repress, however. Feelings have to be worked through and then, at some point, there can be no looking back. "Let not your minds turn back." (D&C 67:14.)

RESTITUTION

As it applies to sin, restitution means to restore or put back that which was stolen and correct whatever damage was done. It applies to weakness, afflictions, and trauma as well as to sin. Restitution is a two-way process. We are asked to restore what we can—not as punishment but as a process of healing. Christ then miraculously restores what we cannot.

My bishop encouraged me to become involved in service projects to make restitution for the sexual sins I had committed. Service was not requested for "payment." Heavenly Father uses charitable acts to provide healing and as a source of pure, divine love for souls who have suffered the effects of unrighteous love.

Elder Dean L. Larsen reviewed studies done among Church members to determine what had a positive influence on their lives. "Three things seem to emerge regularly as having tremendous importance in the acquiring and maintaining of spiritual health and well-being. These may not be surprising to you, and yet may be because they are so standard and foundational to the gospel we don't give them as much attention as we need to. One is *prayer*. . . . The second is the *study of the scriptures*—regular study. . . . The third thing is *a disposition to do something good for someone else,* an inclination to forget self in a concern for someone else. Now, I'm not just talking about church service. Assigned church service is important, but I refer more to an attitude or a disposition to be alert to the needs of others and then the determination to make an effort in some way to respond to those needs. There is apparently something so very Christlike about that attribute that it represents a tremendously strong underpinning of emotional and spiritual strength." (*AMCAP Journal*, vol. 12, no. 2 [1986]: 16–17; italics in original.)

Charity has the power to lift, to establish a sense of divine worth, and to fill needs. It was put into action as a working gospel principle when I performed acts of service in the proper spirit. I started to see past my own world and notice that other people actually had problems, too.

I also learned to restore what I could of the damage that abuse and other difficulties had caused in my life. I began to make up for a lost childhood. I discovered things I had enjoyed as a child—or would have enjoyed as a child. I took a trip to the beach and collected seashells. I bought a mountain bike and a trick kite. I bought myself an occasional ice cream sundae. I started developing, or making up, new talents.

I found strength as I replaced negative behaviors with uplifting ones. "Be not overcome of evil, but overcome evil with good." (Romans 12:21.)

Restoring same-sex friendships and meeting needs

Attractions are brought about by needs. Homosexual fantasy or behavior can become the means to satisfy those needs. Forsaking homosexual relationships causes those feelings and needs to surface. Hence, overcoming involves a process of learning to identify those needs and meeting them in nonsexual ways.

For those who are in a strictly emotionally dependent relationship, it is important to discontinue that relationship and make other friends (more than one). Great care must be taken to keep new friendships in check to avoid other emotional dependencies.

Some have disclosed their homosexual attractions to a same-sex friend and have then become sexually involved with that person. It is important for those who seek freedom from homosexual desires to refrain from disclosing to a person whom, in the back of their mind, they find attractive while secretly hoping the attraction is mutual. Again, honesty with self is very important.

Appropriate same-sex friendships can meet needs that have not been met in the past. It takes time to establish new patterns. At first, "mere" friendships never seem enough. But as needs are gradually met, homosexual desires lessen in intensity. "All of the prayer, insight, and effort you can muster won't change your sexual desires one bit if you don't establish the kind of relationships you need." (Dallas, *Desires in Conflict,* p. 123.)

Appropriate friendships can also provide the comfort of human touch. I had a couple of close friends and a bishop who hugged me when I needed support. The greatest fulfillment I found—even when it came to "feeling" the physical love of another—was from the Savior. As the Spirit of Jesus Christ became more tangible, so did the sense of His comfort.

Restoring gender identity

Some people who struggle with same-sex attraction do not feel comfortable in their identity as a man or a woman. I never wished to be anything other than a woman, but the word *feminine* always bothered me. I had a difficult time with what I thought were society's concepts of masculine and feminine. I felt inferior in my role as a woman, whatever that role was.

I finally learned to look to Jesus Christ, our Example. We are to become like Him, and that is true for both women and men. He has perfected what we often define as masculine traits as well as feminine characteristics. He is strong and determined, a powerful leader. He is also nurturing, sensitive, gentle, and meek.

Finding role models who are comfortable with their gender can help. Many righteous Church leaders have acquired a balance of traits that some tend to categorize as feminine or masculine, while maintaining their own masculinity or femininity.

I looked to the Relief Society General Presidency. They have demolished the stereotype I had of Relief Society sisters—a bunch of willy-nilly old ladies baking bread and sharing exciting new Jell-O recipes over coffee tables adorned with large resin grapes. President Elaine L. Jack talks of hiking in the high mountains with her husband and sons and proclaims to women that "we will change the world. For the better. For this journey to great heights is not any ordinary journey, any more than was Sariah's. Ours is a quest to change ourselves, to become even truer disciples of our Lord and Savior. We will lift our eyes to the mountains and move ceaselessly towards exaltation." ("Look Up and Press On," *Ensign,* May 1992, p. 99.)

I stand corrected.

Members of the Quorum of the Twelve Apostles are kind and gentle. They openly show affection toward other men and are obviously comfortable with their gender identity. I appreciate the truly Christlike love that emanated from Elder Marvin J. Ashton. It was obvious he practiced what he preached: "Imagine what could happen in today's world—or in our own wards, or families, or priesthood quorums and auxiliaries—if each of us would vow to cherish, watch over, and comfort one another. Imagine the possibilities!" ("The Tongue Can Be a Sharp Sword," *Ensign,* May 1992, p. 20.)

Some people who struggle with same-sex attraction may easily develop Christlike traits that others of their same gender may have to work hard to obtain. Unfortunately, that can contribute to feelings of being different, even inferior. A boy who is tenderhearted or gentle might be teased by his peers or by a father who wants to "toughen him up."

I finally learned to embrace strength and forthrightness—often considered masculine traits—and to become more comfortable with feminine qualities. I discovered I'd become somewhat hardened because of the abuse. I viewed sensitivity and gentleness as vulnerabilities and built a hard shell as protection. As I dealt with the abuse, I took my walls down and felt safe to become softer and more sensitive.

Some men find it helpful to get involved with sports or start working out to gain a greater sense of masculinity. Changing certain mannerisms or mode of dress can also help men as well as women. I'm not suggesting people should conform to society's expectations; rather, they can find ways to develop traits that help them feel more comfortable with their own gender.

I believe the greatest results could be achieved if we all encouraged and nurtured "feminine" and "masculine" qualities within everyone, allowing for individual differences.

Restoring attractions toward the opposite sex

Attractions toward the opposite sex often cannot be developed until homosexual desires have been worked through. Heterosexual feelings cannot be forced. Great care must be taken when developing them. A person must be strong enough to handle the new challenges that heterosexual relationships often bring.

It took two years of making serious strides away from homosexual relationships before I could begin working on heterosexual relationships. Even then, bad experiences on dates with men would set me back. I'd start comparing men to women, and men paled in comparison. A bad date would convince me I could never be happy with a man, and I'd resign myself to the "fact" that I would be lonely the rest of my life. I'd even take it a step further and decide that since I disliked dating men, I must be permanently gay.

One important key to restoring opposite-sex attraction has been the realization that it truly is a restoration. God's plan for eternal life requires the union of man and woman. His plan is also the plan of happiness, although circumstances can make that difficult or impossible to believe. The knowledge and acceptance of God's plan has increased my faith that not only can I get married but I can experience happiness within marriage.

In order for me to develop opposite-sex attractions, it was extremely important to stop considering homosexual relationships as options. I had to shift my focus completely. I became willing to devote the time and energy required to build healthy heterosexual relationships. Unlike my attractions toward women—which developed without any effort and continued to surface even when I tried to ignore them—I had to struggle to find and develop attractions toward men.

I worked with a counselor on feelings and conflicts as they arose while dating. Although I'd always gotten along fine with men, I was rather indifferent toward them in dating situations. I learned that what I thought was indifference toward men was really a cover for my anger. As I worked through the anger, I discovered fear was buried underneath.

The process has been involved. Over the years, however, my feelings and attractions toward men have continually changed for the better (despite the claim of some professionals that it is impossible). The most significant changes in my attractions toward the opposite sex have come through the power of heaven as I have done all I can do. That has happened because the Holy Spirit "increases, enlarges, expands, and purifies all the natural passions and affections, and adapts them, by the gift of wisdom, to their lawful use." (Parley P. Pratt, *Key to the Science of Theology* [Salt Lake City: Deseret Book Co., 1965], p. 101.)

The greatest restoration

As we take even a single step to restore our lives, Jesus Christ goes to the edge of eternity and back. Whether it's sin or weakness or trauma, it is impossible for us to make restitution by ourselves.

Sexual sin is not the only sin for which we cannot make total restitution by ourselves. We cannot call idle gossip back. A broken Sabbath cannot be repaired. Even something that appears to have been restored—twenty dollars is stolen and returned—is not fully restored. Repayment of the twenty dollars does not pay for the sin.

Christ's message is that He will pay our price. Even if our past is full of sin, He can restore all.

For many years, because of the sexual molestations, I believed I had lost my virtue and could never gain it back. Even though I was later sexually involved and morally responsible for that involvement, that still did not mean I had lost my virtue permanently. The good news of the gospel is that we can all find virtue again. The vilest of sinners can become the holiest of saints.

My virtue has been restored. And there is no doubt as to whom I am eternally indebted. "Jesus said, Somebody hath touched me: for I perceive that virtue is gone out of me. And when the woman saw that she was not hid, she came trembling, and falling down before him, she declared unto him before all the people for what cause she had touched him, and how she was healed immediately. And he said unto her, Daughter, be of good comfort: thy faith hath made thee whole; go in peace." (Luke 8:46–48.)

Christ also performs miracles to meet our needs and heal our pains and our afflictions. One night, after years of working through the abuse, I was talking with a friend about the day I set the kitten

and my childhood down. Feeling more of the grief and the guilt and
the horrible pain associated with the abuse, I closed my eyes and
could see Christ walk over to me as a thirteen-year-old girl and put
His arms around me. He "took their little children, one by one, and
blessed them, and prayed unto the Father for them . . . and they saw
angels descending out of heaven as it were in the midst of fire; and
they came down and encircled those little ones about, and they were
encircled about with fire; and the angels did minister unto them."
(3 Nephi 17:21, 24.)

After I had taken the necessary time to work through the emotions and release them, Christ took them up. He restored my frac-
tured life.

FORGIVENESS

In addition to forgiveness from heaven, which is paramount, I
discovered two important aspects of forgiveness that were vital to my
healing. One was forgiving myself and the other was forgiving those
who had offended me or who I thought had offended me.

Forgiveness of self

I often forgave myself last, when I desperately needed that forgiveness at the first. Satan twists everything. Guilt was designed to
bring about a desire to change, not a desire to commit suicide. Self-
hatred is not part of Heavenly Father's plan.

Just as we are entreated to love ourselves, we are also asked to
forgive ourselves. "Of you it is required to forgive all men [and
women]." (D&C 64:10.) This commandment includes ourselves. It
was presumptuous to think I could decide whether or not I was forgiven when Christ had told me, through an appointed judge in
Israel, that I had been forgiven. We are to listen to the Lord's anointed and not overrule God's judgments, considering ourselves to be
the supreme judges.

I realize now it was not correct thinking, but without feeling forgiveness, I had difficulty finding a reason not to sin again. I still felt
guilty and despised for the sins I'd committed previously. How much
more guilty could I be?

"Behold, he who has repented of his sins, the same is forgiven, and I, the Lord, remember them no more." (D&C 58:42.) It's just as important that we let them go.

Sometimes I would go for months or years without committing a particular sin. Then if I slipped up, I would berate myself and feel terribly guilty, even suicidal. I would be convinced I was right back where I had started from and that I had never really changed. In reality, I had gained much from time spent abstaining. I finally took that into account and became more forgiving of myself.

I also stopped beating myself up for having homosexual feelings in the first place. I used to blame myself for having such attractions. And although I needed to forgive myself for feeding those desires and acting upon them, there was no need to seek forgiveness for being a person who was facing the challenge of same-sex attraction. I had no control over that.

Forgiveness of others

Forgiving other people occurred after I recognized and expressed the feelings that were attached to the offenses. I finally accepted the love my mother has for me and understood that she did her absolute best in raising me. She'd made the mistake of being human. I realized I was guilty of the same offense of which I had accused her: I did not accept her for who she was. We have both worked at improving our relationship. Healing and restoration has come as a result. The pressure was also taken off the relationship when I began to feel unconditional love and approval from my heavenly parents. Their perfect love met some of the needs that were not met by my earthly parents.

Many suffer from far more serious offenses committed against them by their parents and others: emotional, physical and/or sexual abuse, neglect, or abandonment. Although some of those relationships cannot be repaired—and often the attempt should not even be made because of the further damage it can cause—it is important to forgive and let go after the feelings have been dealt with.

I finally forgave the man who raped me. For quite some time I thought I'd already forgiven him because I'd say, "He was probably abused as a child, too. I can't really blame him." And that seemed to be that. Then one day I reached a deeper layer and hit the core of my feelings about the abuse. I unleashed anger in a way I never had before. I beat on my couch and screamed at the abuser as if he were there. I told him to get out of my life once and for all. I felt real anger toward him for the first time. I found the power to say no. The Spirit and I finally reclaimed control of my own life and soul.

The promptings to forgive came later. The task was a difficult one. I realized what I had thought was forgiveness was just a way of protecting myself. A crust of cooled lava had covered the molten lava seething below. Now I had broken through to the anger.

My mind hit overload as I tried to make sense of why someone would destroy my childhood and wreak havoc on my life just so he could find some twisted kind of sexual pleasure for a few minutes. I thought forgiveness could only come after I had made sense of it. Everything kept going round and round and round and round and round in my head till I thought I would explode.

The Spirit and a friend helped me find the solution. I would never be able to make sense of it, nor was I expected to. I needed to let it go.

Previously, forgiveness had always come from understanding. This time it could not. I took the whole tangled mess and gave it to the Lord. I was finally released from the galling chains of abuse that had kept me bound for so many years.

Forgiveness of others is for our own benefit, not the offender's. In an eternal sense, it is the Lord's forgiveness that matters, and He makes those decisions: "I, the Lord, will forgive whom I will forgive, but of you it is required to forgive all men." (D&C 64:10.) I found the best way to look at it was not as "forgiving," which often connotes absolving in an eternal sense. It is impossible for us to absolve anyone from sin in that sense.

Forgiveness of others is really more of a letting go. Anger, resentment, and other feelings that can bind a person to the effects of the offense need to be abandoned at some point. To hold something against another person means to hold onto something. Complete wholeness cannot be restored when negative feelings stand in the way.

Our Heavenly Father's request that we forgive is made out of love and compassion for us—that we might be set free. Forgiveness is for us.

KEEPING THE COMMANDMENTS

I came to realize I could not compensate for homosexual behavior or alcoholism by doing other good works. I remember thinking, "As long as I do all these other things right, it should be OK. I'm still a good person. There's just this one thing." I learned it was necessary to strive to keep all the commandments. And keeping all the commandments I could gave me the strength to keep others.

I gained a greater awareness of the charge to "love the Lord thy God with all thy heart, and with all thy soul, and with all thy mind, and with all thy strength." (Mark 12:30.) We must become emotionally, spiritually, mentally, and physically devoted to Him. He is well aware of the importance of those four areas in maintaining balance.

Emotionally, I learned to build strong, healthy friendships to help fill my needs. I began to feel more and more comfortable at church. I have not changed my personality. I've come closer to Christ, which in turn has helped me feel closer to fellow Christians. I've gone from feeling an outcast at Relief Society to feeling the true spirit of sisterhood and a strong sense of belonging. Friends accept me because of and in spite of my differences.

Spiritually, I did all I could to strengthen my faith, much of which I have already described. I realized we aren't supposed to be perfect before we go to the temple—the temple helps perfect us. Temple attendance increased my spiritual strength tremendously. There are forces that work in the temple with greater intensity than anywhere else on earth.

Spending time outdoors also brought spiritual strength. The wonder of creation intrigues me. I am not surprised that when people are taught the gospel, the story of the Creation is an integral part.

Mentally, I began searching through books as I searched for ways out of homosexual relationships. I became better acquainted with myself and the workings of the Spirit by keeping a journal of feelings and impressions. I could look back and see what I was feeling before I felt compelled to make a visit or a phone call I shouldn't have made. I exerted mental energy toward figuring out what made things easier or more difficult. I marked my progress, be it ever so slow. During the tough times, I looked back to records of spiritually strengthening experiences, and that provided the sustenance I needed to carry me through the famine.

I was careful not to focus too much on the subject of same-sex attraction. We are asked to "seek ye out of the best books words of wisdom; seek learning, even by study and also by faith." (D&C 88:118.) I replaced thinking about homosexual desires with constructive learning. I found that the more mentally engaging and challenging the activity, the greater power it had to take my mind off same-sex attraction. Concentrating on other activities was much easier than concentrating on refraining from thinking about homosexual desires.

Physically, I found aerobic exercises I enjoyed so that I was more likely to maintain a consistent workout program. Current research indicates that half an hour of exercise three times a week helps reduce stress. Exercise was extremely helpful as I overcame alcoholism. It is also very important for anyone trying to overcome sexual dependency and other addictive behaviors.

The body is not to be ignored. It is our vehicle to godhood. Eating right, maintaining a healthy weight, and getting proper rest are also essential. We receive promises at the end of the Word of Wisdom, after the Lord admonishes us to avoid alcohol and tobacco and to eat right. The physical promises that we "shall run and not be weary, and shall walk and not faint" make perfect sense. We are also promised that we "shall find wisdom and great treasures of knowledge, even hidden treasures." (See D&C 89:19–20.) Living the Word of Wisdom helps unite body and spirit, bringing the true self to the forefront.

TRUE FREEDOM FROM THE NATURAL SELF

C. S. Lewis has stated that Christ asks us to "'hand over the whole natural self, all the desires which you think innocent as well as the ones you think wicked—the whole outfit. I will give you a new self instead. In fact, I will give you Myself: my own will shall become yours.'" (*Mere Christianity* [New York: Macmillan, 1943], p. 167.)

Repentance is a wondrous process. It is the means whereby mortals can shed the natural self that pulls us downward and be lifted up towards godhood by a greater power.

CHAPTER 9

BAPTISM AND THE SACRAMENT

Yea, I say unto you come and fear not, and lay aside every sin, which easily doth beset you, which doth bind you down to destruction, yea, come and go forth, and show unto your God that ye are willing to repent of your sins and enter into a covenant with him to keep his commandments, and witness it unto him this day by going into the waters of baptism." (Alma 7:15.)

I had to completely immerse my natural self so my life could be cleansed from sin and sinful desires. To become a new creature in Christ, I had to "die" to my old ways. "Therefore we are buried with him by baptism into death: that like as Christ was raised up from the dead by the glory of the Father, even so we also should walk in newness of life. . . . Knowing this, that our old man is crucified with him, that the body of sin might be destroyed, that henceforth we should not serve sin." (Romans 6:4, 6.)

Symbolizing Christ's life, death, and resurrection, baptism also represents the death and burial of the natural self (the "old man" or "body of sin") and the resurrection of the new self.

Part of the reason it took so long for me to immerse my natural self is that I kept insisting on sticking my toe out of the water. I stubbornly held onto desires, "innocent" remembrances of times gone by and occasional "harmless" phone calls. Wandering thoughts continued to provide some satisfaction and enjoyment. But to bury my natural self, I had to stop all that so a total immersion could occur.

"Repent, all ye ends of the earth, and come unto me and be baptized in my name, that ye may be sanctified by the reception of the Holy Ghost." (3 Nephi 27:20.) The literal baptism by water is a onetime event, except for Church members who have been excommunicated. But the remission or complete cleansing of sin occurs throughout our lives. The sacrament provides a way for us to renew the covenants or promises we made at baptism and to be cleansed through Christ's atonement. Each of the three sacramental covenants has become deeply meaningful to me. (See D&C 20:77, 79.)

The first covenant is that *"they are willing to take upon them the name of thy Son."* The world would have us take upon ourselves lesser names. Even Alcoholics Anonymous, a program I credit with helping me overcome alcoholism, teaches a person to admit he's an "alcoholic" the rest of his life. I suppose that is to remind her or him they can never be social drinkers and to help them remember they will always be dependent upon their "higher power."

Heavenly Father and Jesus Christ—our higher power—want us to take upon ourselves a greater name. "And moreover, I say unto you, that there shall be no other name given nor any other way nor means whereby salvation can come unto the children of men, only in and through the name of Christ, the Lord Omnipotent." (Mosiah 3:17.)

I finally stopped calling myself a "homosexual" or an "alcoholic." Instead of identifying with my weaknesses, I began identifying with my Strength. I no longer depend on homosexual relationships or on alcohol. I depend on Jesus Christ. I have made a covenant, and I renew it every week, that I will not be known through any name other than Christ's.

The second sacramental covenant, *"always remember him,"* helped me redirect my thoughts. I began turning my attention away from sin and towards Christ. When thoughts entered my mind I knew shouldn't be there, I would replace them with the Spirit through prayer or scripture study. As I continued to turn my thoughts toward heaven, my heart started to follow.

Obeying the third sacramental covenant, to *"keep his commandments,"* came about incrementally. I learned to concentrate on gospel covenants that were within my grasp. Great power came as I made and kept promises at every level of progression. They carried even greater power when I was able to bind them with such gospel ordinances as the sacrament and then temple ordinances.

Covenants represent a two-way promise. If we obey covenants, Heavenly Father and Christ are bound, and pleased, to bestow blessings upon us as their part of the covenant. "I, the Lord, am bound when ye do what I say; but when ye do not what I say, ye have no promise." (D&C 82:10.)

Additional strength to make changes in my life has come from physically and spiritually taking part in covenants through the sacrament and in the temple. I believe this strength is due, in part, to our bodies and spirits being particularly united in purpose and deed during these ordinances as long as we are spiritually, emotionally, and physically prepared to participate. The sacrament is blessed and sanctified *"to the souls of all those who partake of it."* And "the spirit and the body are the soul of man." (D&C 88:15.)

I do not yet fully understand covenants and ordinances, but I have become more and more aware of the power they bring. Covenants bind us to the power of God, affording us the freedom to become who we truly are.

By obeying the sacramental covenants, I have felt the marvelous effects of the Lord's part of the covenant, that *"they may always have his Spirit to be with them."* Christ's presence becomes more tangible when I physically and spiritually partake of the emblems that symbolize His flesh and blood. Not only does the ordinance unite my spirit and body in a unique way but it symbolizes the unification of my soul with His.

When I've made the effort to repent and properly prepare myself, I sit in awe, gratefully, humbly, on a padded bench in a house of the Lord and sip the clear water from a small plastic cup passed to me by an Aaronic priesthood holder. The emblems take me back to where the Church of today got its meaning. As I sip from the pristine cup, I can see Christ in the Garden, deserted by His closest companions, writhing in agony and bleeding from every pore. He collapses under the weight of the world and cries, "O my Father, if it be possible, let this cup pass from me: nevertheless not as I will, but as thou wilt." And, as I stay carefully in tune, it is not the Aaronic priesthood holder's steps I notice but those of the Roman guards, here at Golgotha, the place of the skull. With them is my Savior, wearing a crown of platted thorns and the spit of humankind. They put Him upon a cross far greater than any I have ever borne. His hands are nailed in place. As His flesh rips, they put nails in His wrists. Then they strip Him of His raiment but never of His dignity. For as they read in mocking, so it is true from eternity to all eternity: THIS IS JESUS OF NAZARETH THE KING OF THE JEWS. Then it goes dark. The earth is swallowed up with a bleakness she has never known. From the void comes, not a still small voice but an agonizing cry: "Eloi, Eloi, lama sabachthani?" which is, being interpreted, "My God, my God, why hast thou forsaken me?" After being given a sponge full of vinegar, Christ decides it is time. "Father, into thy hands I commend my spirit." And it was so. (See Matthew 26–27; Mark 15; Luke 23; John 19.)

"Heavenly Father, please help me remember Him and keep His commandments so I can always have His Spirit to be with me."

CHAPTER 10

THE MIGHTY CHANGE

In 1845, the Franklin expedition set sail in two ships from England in search of a northwest passage through the Arctic to the Pacific Ocean. Each sailing vessel contained a backup steam engine and enough coal for the ship to run on auxiliary power for twelve days—that was in preparation for a voyage that was expected to take up to three years. Apparently, rather than storing extra coal, they brought along provisions for their own immediate comfort. Included on board were a hand organ, china place settings, wine glasses, and ornate sterling silverware with large, solid handles engraved with the officers' initials and family crests.

None of the 138 men returned alive. Instead, their remains were later discovered at various places across the frozen Arctic. One group from the Franklin expedition had apparently taken off in search of civilization. There among the frozen bodies, among those men who were desperately tracking through life-threatening conditions, was the heavy, engraven silverware they'd been hauling across the frozen wasteland.

Looking back on my life from an eternal perspective, I see my past in much the same way. At the time, homosexual relationships were very valuable and precious. There seemed to be little reason to continue life's journey without them.

Now I have a grander outlook. Having experienced a mighty change in my life, I recognize those relationships for what they were. I can see that they halted my spiritual progression. Holding onto them meant losing my life—my eternal life. From an eternal viewpoint, I see them as nothing more than polished silver.

The world can continue to claim that "homosexuals" cannot change, but that is the worldly perspective. An eternal perspective unveils the grand possibilities of growth and change for every living soul.

Once considered a "homosexual," I have changed in many ways. I, like the people of King Benjamin, believe the words that have been spoken by the prophets and "know of their surety and truth, because of the Spirit of the Lord Omnipotent, which has wrought a mighty change in [me], or in [my heart], that [I] have no more disposition to do evil, but to do good continually." I am "willing to enter into a covenant with [my] God to do his will, and to be obedient to his commandments in all things that he shall command [me], all the remainder of [my] days." For I "say that [my heart has been] changed through faith on his name; therefore, [I am] born of him and have become his [daughter]." (Mosiah 5:2, 5, 7.)

WHAT IT MEANS TO BE BORN OF GOD

Of all the gospel principles, being born of God has been the most difficult for me to understand. It is spoken of as the mighty change, being converted, being born again, becoming the children of Christ, being spiritually reborn, baptized by fire and being filled with the Holy Ghost. It is different from the actual laying on of hands to receive the gift of the Holy Ghost. "Besides the physical ordinance of baptism and the laying on of hands, one must be spiritually born again to gain exaltation and eternal life." (Ezra Taft Benson, "Born of God," *Ensign*, Nov. 1985, p. 6.)

Many accounts in the Book of Mormon describe spiritual rebirth as an event and show that part of the process occurs while the people are in a trance or a state of unconsciousness. (See Alma 18–19; 22.) Even the people of King Benjamin referred to a sudden realization that a mighty change had been wrought in their hearts.

But the mighty change is not usually a singular event; rather, it is often a gradual process that includes a confirming witness of the Holy Spirit. Moroni summarizes the process: "And the first fruits of repentance is baptism; and baptism cometh by faith unto the fulfilling the commandments; and the fulfilling the commandments bringeth remission of sins; and the remission of sins bringeth

meekness, and lowliness of heart; and because of meekness and lowliness of heart cometh the visitation of the Holy Ghost, which
Comforter filleth with hope and perfect love." (Moroni 8:25–26.)

My process of becoming born of God started with the light of
hope and was added upon through faith, repentance, and the renewing of baptismal covenants. Gradually I was filled with the light of
the Holy Spirit. A confirming witness of the mighty change came
years after I had begun to abstain from homosexual behavior and
emotionally binding relationships. I am certain it is not by chance
that my experience with baptism by fire occurred the night I was
praying to Heavenly Father to offer up what had become a distant
friendship with Tracy.

Then there's Alma who was busy leading the people "away unto
destruction" when he experienced the mighty change. We don't
know what else he might have experienced before his spiritual awak-
ening, or what he might have gone through during his two days and
two nights of soul-searching. (See Mosiah 27:23.)

The mighty change may not be as immediate and noticeable as it
was for Alma, nor is it a rare occurrence reserved for a select few.
President Ezra Taft Benson has said: "For every Paul, for every Enos,
and for every King Lamoni, there are hundreds and thousands of
people who find the process of repentance more subtle, much more
imperceptible. Day by day they move closer to the Lord, little realizing they are building a godlike life. They are like the Lamanites,
who the Lord said 'were baptized with fire and with the Holy Ghost,
and they knew it not.' (3 Nephi 9:20; italics added.)" (*Repentance* [Salt
Lake City: Deseret Book Co., 1990], pp. 6–7.)

We should all seek to be born of God—in this life. "Marvel not
that all mankind, yea, men and women, all nations, kindreds,
tongues and people, must be born again; yea, born of God, changed
from their carnal and fallen state, to a state of righteousness, being
redeemed of God, becoming his sons and daughters; and thus they
become new creatures; and unless they do this, they can in nowise
inherit the kingdom of God." (Mosiah 27:25–26.) The mighty
change is an integral part of the gospel and is expounded upon in
John 3; Acts 4:31–32; Mosiah 3–5, 27; Alma 5, 18–19, 22, 26, 32,
36; and Moses 6.

Jesus tells us, "Verily, verily, I say unto thee, Except a man be born again, he cannot see the kingdom of God." (John 3:3.) Modern-day Church leaders have reiterated the importance of becoming born of God. President David O. McKay told of having a vision in which he saw people dressed in white abiding with the Savior in the "City Eternal." Above them appeared the words "These Are They Who Have Overcome the World—Who Have Truly Been Born Again!" (*Cherished Experiences from the Writings of President David O. McKay*, comp. Clare Middlemiss [Salt Lake City: Deseret Book Co., 1955], p. 102.)

THE SPIRITUAL REBIRTH

Adam was taught that "inasmuch as ye were born into the world by water, and blood, and the spirit, which I have made, and so became of dust a living soul, even so ye must be born again into the kingdom of heaven, of water, and of the Spirit, and be cleansed by blood, even the blood of mine Only Begotten; that ye might be sanctified from all sin, and enjoy the words of eternal life in this world, and eternal life in the world to come, even immortal glory." (Moses 6:59.)

Being born into the kingdom of God is directly comparable to being born into this mortal world. Gerald N. Lund explains the comparison: "As it was with our first birth, so it is when we are 'born again.' Water, blood, and Spirit are again essential. In the water of the baptismal font, we are again totally immersed in a watery environment. In other words, the baptismal font is not only a symbol of the grave, where we bury the old sinful man, but also a symbol of the womb where the newborn spiritual person is given life. The atoning blood of Christ is also required, and like the blood in our bodies, the atoning blood nourishes, cleanses, and protects us from spiritual infection. And finally, the source of life for the reborn spiritual man is the Holy Spirit. If it were not so, the newborn spiritual man would be 'stillborn.'" (*Jesus Christ, Key to the Plan of Salvation* [Salt Lake City: Deseret Book Co., 1991], p. 107.)

The natural self is sent to a watery grave at baptism, and the impure part of us is burned off through the baptism of fire or the Holy Spirit. We become spiritually reborn. We "[put] off the natural man and [become] a saint through the atonement of Christ the Lord, and [become] as a child" (Mosiah 3:19)—a child born of God. The Holy Spirit is the means by which our true, spiritual self gains complete freedom and power to act. We are made alive through the Holy Ghost in the attributes of our true self. "And thus [Adam] was baptized, and the Spirit of God descended upon him, and thus he was born of the Spirit, and became quickened in the inner man." (Moses 6:65.) He was made alive in his true self.

FROM CARNAL NATURE TO DIVINE NATURE

What we may previously have claimed to be a permanent part of our nature is changed through the process of spiritual rebirth. Even if desires are directed toward homosexual relationships as part of the human nature, spiritual rebirth into the kingdom of God causes desires to become directed toward righteousness as part of the divine nature. "Whereby are given unto us exceeding great and precious promises: that by these ye might be partakers of the divine nature, having escaped the corruption that is in the world through lust." (2 Peter 1:4.)

President David O. McKay stated: "No man can sincerely resolve to apply to his daily life the teachings of Jesus of Nazareth without sensing a change in his own nature. The phrase 'born again,' has a deeper significance than many people attach to it." (In Conference Report, Apr. 1962, p. 7.) And President Ezra Taft Benson declared, "The world would shape human behavior, but Christ can change human nature." ("Born of God," *Ensign*, Nov. 1985, p. 6.)

To be born of God means to become aware of our heavenly parents' attributes within us as we identify with our divine nature instead of our human nature. For example, I've grown increasingly aware of my ability, and my desire, to marry by the "new and everlasting covenant" and to abide in that covenant. I used to talk about a temple marriage "someday," but in day-to-day life it was far from my feelings and actions. Now it no longer seems to go against my nature.

Since I've become spiritually motivated in all things, my desire to be married has been strengthened. "For I, the Lord God, created all things, of which I have spoken, spiritually, before they were naturally upon the face of the earth." (Moses 3:5.) I have made the greatest strides in developing attractions toward the opposite sex since I began to desire righteousness as part of my divine nature. My attractions toward men are becoming founded on a spiritual basis.

CHARITY IS THE GREATEST GIFT OF THE HOLY SPIRIT

Charity comes from experiencing the mighty change and being filled with the Holy Spirit. Moroni tells us that after faith, repentance, and the remission of sins, the Holy Ghost "filleth with hope and perfect love." (Moroni 8:26.) It comes as a reward of faith unto repentance, making it the "end of the commandment." (1 Timothy 1:5.) The reward of nourishing the seed of faith is its fruit, the love of God and Christ: "By and by ye shall pluck the fruit thereof, which is most precious, which is sweet above all that is sweet, and which is white above all that is white, yea, and pure above all that is pure." (Alma 32:42.)

Being born of God and partaking of His love brings indescribable joy and fulfillment. Alma sought to "bring souls unto repentance; that I might bring them to taste of the exceeding joy of which I did taste; that they might also be born of God, and be filled with the Holy Ghost." (Alma 36:24.) Nephi taught that the love of God "sheddeth itself abroad in the hearts of the children of men; wherefore, it is the most desirable above all things. And he spake unto me, saying: Yea, and the most joyous to the soul." (1 Nephi 11:21–23.)

By partaking of charity, we become "partakers of [our] divine nature." The saying "The apple doesn't fall far from the tree" usually applies to children taking on the characteristics and actions of their earthly parents. It acknowledges the role genetics and environment play in shaping our lives. But this analogy with an earthly family tree applies more eternally and permanently to the tree of life. If we become born of God and partake of the fruit of the tree of life—of God's love—we take on the characteristics and actions of Christ and our heavenly parents.

Alma asks, "Have ye spiritually been born of God? Have ye received his image in your countenance?" (Alma 5:14.) By becoming born of God and filled with charity, we become like Christ because Christ is love. As Bernard of Clairvaux said, "What we love we shall grow to resemble."

THE MIGHTY CHANGE REQUIRES MIGHTY EFFORT

More times than I care to admit I've complained to heaven about the amount of effort I've had to put forth to overcome sin. I'd look at other Church members and say, "Hey, how come they don't have to exercise all the time and go to the temple every week and only watch Disney films and read 'spiritually uplifting' material every day, and blah, blah, blah?"

The truth is, anyone who has experienced the mighty change has done so by going to a great deal of effort. If some of them fall, it's usually only into mediocrity rather than into some all-consuming, destructive behavior.

But mediocrity has perils of its own. "So then because thou art lukewarm, and neither cold nor hot, I will spue thee out of my mouth." (Revelation 3:16.) The tricky part about becoming lukewarm is that the temperature usually falls slowly and unnoticeably. It can be difficult to recognize the gradual descent.

I'm grateful I have a built-in thermometer that is highly sensitive, so that I can tell immediately when I'm off half a degree and I can quickly correct whatever I'm doing wrong.

Consistent, dedicated effort is required of anyone who seeks to maintain a state of being spiritually reborn. The people who formed the model society in Fourth Nephi were born of God. There was "no contention in the land, because of the love of God which did dwell in the hearts of the people." (4 Nephi 1:15.) Hugh Nibley suggests that this society disintegrated because "it was too strenuous; it required great mental exertion: they spent their time constantly in meetings and prayer and fasting—in concentrating on things (4 Nephi 1:12). The exercise of the mind was simply too exhausting. It was less wearying just to give up and let things drift, to go back to the old ways." (*Temple and Cosmos* [Salt Lake City: Deseret Book Co., 1992], p. 13.)

It is important to study about the mighty change, to pursue it by following the commandments, and to pray to experience it.

People who are tormented by sinful desires or weaknesses, by past trials or traumatic events, can find peace for their souls by becoming born of God.

My desire to follow the entire plan of salvation has been strengthened as my desire to live contrary to Heavenly Father's will has been eliminated. As the people of King Lamoni who were born again witnessed, "their hearts had been changed; that they had no more desire to do evil." (Alma 19:33.) I no longer desire to sin.

Of course I still make mistakes, but in less severe ways than before, and I get back on track quickly. To pull me down, temptations need a part of me to grab onto. With the Lord's help, the "homosexual" and "alcoholic" part of me has been put to rest. Resisting the occasional buffetings of Satan from without is so much easier than constantly resisting desires from within. I spent years struggling to resist desires. And, because of that persistence, I now desire righteousness more than anything else. I have found peace. Thinking about or wishing for or missing sin would destroy the peace that is finally mine. Now that I've found it, I'm not about to let Satan take it away. I refuse to join him in his eternal misery.

The mighty change has allowed me the privilege of enjoying the exquisite opposites of the negative extremes in my life. Inexpressible misery has been turned to inexpressible joy. Torment has been turned to peace. Utter darkness has been filled with light. And loneliness has been filled with immeasurable love.

Yes, even those who have been considered "homosexual" can change. And I, for one, will never go back. I can say with Alma, "After wading through much tribulation, repenting nigh unto death, the Lord in mercy hath seen fit to snatch me out of an everlasting burning, and I am born of God. My soul hath been redeemed from the gall of bitterness and bonds of iniquity. I was in the darkest abyss; but now I behold the marvelous light of God. My soul was racked with eternal torment; but I am snatched, and my soul is pained no more." (Mosiah 27:28–29.)

As President Benson has said, "May we be convinced that Jesus is the Christ, choose to follow Him, be changed for Him, captained by Him, consumed in Him, and born again." ("Born of God," *Ensign,* Nov. 1985, p. 7.)

CHAPTER 11

HEADED HOME

One of the most burdensome aspects of working on this book has been my continued involvement with the issue of same-sex attraction. Once I started on it, I was talking about, thinking about, reading about, and writing about homosexual attraction and meeting with counselors and priesthood leaders—daily. It has become obvious to me—in case it wasn't already—that, at some point, it's all better left behind and moved beyond. After three years of research and writing, I cannot say how grateful I am to have reached this final chapter. I'm definitely ready to close the book.

That is, in part, why I wish to remain behind the scenes, at least for now. Not only do I wish to avoid the label "homosexual" but I also want to avoid the label of "recovered homosexual." It's the same word, only with an adjective attached. Of course, that is my personal wish. I have a much stronger desire to do anything and everything Heavenly Father requires of me. If He asks that I continue to help others overcome same-sex attraction, I will do so. For now, though, I'm hoping this book will suffice. You won't find me at your local LDS bookstore serving truffles and signing books.

In describing the process of gaining freedom from same-sex attraction, I have tried not to lose sight of the true focus—Jesus Christ. He was the source of my healing and is the everlasting Source of my strength. "Yea, I know that I am nothing; as to my strength I am weak; therefore I will not boast of myself, but I will boast of my God, for in his strength I can do all things." (Alma 26:12.)

Rather than saying I'm nothing without Jesus Christ, perhaps I should say that I am everything without Him: "I am an alcoholic. I am a homosexual. I am a victim of sexual abuse." The list goes on and on. But with Him, and because of Him, I am none of those things. I am a daughter of Christ.

There is a power that moves this universe with splendor and grandeur. It makes the earth rotate on its axis and revolve around the sun. It is the same force that daily shapes canyons and glaciers. And human lives. It makes those lives a little less human and a little more godlike with each sweeping motion. We must make ourselves a part of that movement. Not on our terms but on the Lord's. Commandments must be obeyed. Just as planets are kept aligned by this mighty force and prevented from shooting off in all directions and exploding into chaos, so must we align ourselves with the same governing principles. Our world must revolve around the Son.

I am grateful to play a part in helping the gospel roll forth. I am no longer unhappy or unfulfilled. I am no longer denying my true self. The peace I now feel is the deepest, truest part of who I am.

I don't know precisely when I went from being convinced I was a "homosexual" who would never find happiness outside of a same-sex relationship to knowing I am a daughter of Christ who can only find joy in righteousness. I'm not sure when I went from hearing heaven's music as "out-of-tune" singing by Church leaders to hearing it for what it is, an eternal melody that carries with it the familiarity of home. My true home.

Now, my life is finally in harmony. I'm headed home with the kind of determination and faith that move a mountain of weaknesses and divide a sea of troubles. I can no longer be distracted, although Satan tries his best with second-best. As I rise above my circumstances, others shout, "Hey, get back down here. You're gay—you were born that way!" A television advertisement flashes an ice cold six-pack of beer. The stores display a hundred different things my tithing money could buy. Even my thoughts seek to turn against me.

But "if God be for us, who [or what] can be against us?" (Romans 8:31.) "How excellent is thy lovingkindness, O God! therefore [I shall] put [my] trust under the shadow of thy wings." (Psalm 36:7.)

The power to rise above mortal circumstance is not reserved for a select few. I testify that although the challenge to find freedom from the natural self can be extremely difficult, it is not impossible.

The notes are falling into place. Whatever Heavenly Father asks me to do, I will obey. Giving Him the baton has given rise to perfect harmony.

It is Heavenly Father who orchestrates my life. I urge others to follow His call to come home.

CHAPTER 12

To Friends, Families, and Leaders

I will never forget the day Brother Reeves spoke in our ward after he had suffered a tragic accident that left him paralyzed. Someone wheeled him up the the aisle, through the midst of the congregation, to the microphone that had been specially prepared. All eyes were upon him, and most of them were moist. The last time we had seen him approach the pulpit, he had walked with his own two legs.

He thanked all of us in the ward for our support, for the cards and letters and flowers, for the home-cooked meals that had been lovingly prepared, for the help with the yard work and the household chores. "We couldn't have made it through without your help."

The entire congregation was still. Everyone was listening intently, closely wrapped in the silence.

Suddenly I thought, "What does this remind me of? The silence, the Church members, the testimony . . . "

That was it! The Sunday, years before, when I had attended Relief Society and wished I could stand up and say that I was struggling with homosexual desires and alcoholism and that I needed help. Yet, I refrained from speaking, fearing my words would bring a deafening, empty silence.

I remembered going home after that lonely Relief Society meeting, throwing myself on the bed, and crying hysterically at the futility of it all. I stayed in bed the rest of the day. All of the next day, too.

I thought about the woman struggling with homosexual desires I had spoken with that morning, just before hearing Brother Reeves. I thought about all the other people in similar circumstances I had told, "It is very important that you open up to people who are

Church members, who have the Spirit. They can help guide you and offer genuine, Christlike love. But be very selective about whom you tell. Pray about it. Be certain they are true Christians. If they are, they will accept you and strive to give you unconditional love."

How I wished I didn't have to speak such a warning. I wondered how we could be so sympathetic with one trial we have never experienced, such as Brother Reeves' paralysis, and so critical of another. Is it because the details of same-sex attraction are repulsive to most people? Certainly the details of caring for a person who is completely paralyzed are rather unpleasant. Are such details incompatible with compassion? Or is it because people view those with homosexual attractions as having chosen them while Brother Reeves is seen as being the victim of an accident?

Of course, many people in the Church act with compassion toward individuals struggling with homosexual feelings. There may be incidents of condemnation and rejection, but there are also stories of compassion and concern.

Greater understanding and humility before our Heavenly Father can enhance our capacity to love and accept each other, regardless of our trials. Whether we struggle with judgmental, condemning thoughts or homosexual thoughts or both, we need to support one another's efforts to come unto Christ. At baptism we covenanted to "mourn with those that mourn; yea, and comfort those that stand in need of comfort." (Mosiah 18:9.)

"Gay" jokes and similar comments may not be intended to hurt anyone, but we may never know who has struggled with what. I'd been going back to church for about a year and was still on very shaky ground when the ward I was attending presented a slide show. They'd taken a picture of me and another woman at a ward activity (the only other activity I'd mustered up the courage to attend besides the one where they were having this presentation). When the narrator came to that picture, he made a joke about our being a couple. Looking back, I'm sure he had no idea of my situation. I didn't laugh. I was devastated. I went home in a panic, certain the whole ward knew about me and had been making a lot more jokes behind my back. I decided never to return to church. Thankfully, the bishop and a good friend convinced me to do otherwise.

Some might say I shouldn't have taken the incident so personally, but I had already spent years fearing ridicule and rejection. It's difficult for people in the thick of their private battles not to be affected negatively by jokes or other demeaning remarks.

I've heard some negative comments at church concerning those involved in the homosexual lifestyle. One teacher said, "Certainly money should be spent on AIDS research to help those innocent children who suffer, but then there are those . . . " More than once I've heard the misperception expressed that AIDS is somehow deserved, a just punishment for those who have been involved in homosexual relationships.

The scripture states: "Perhaps thou shalt say: The man has brought upon himself his misery; therefore I will stay my hand, and will not give unto him of my food, nor impart unto him of my substance that he may not suffer, for his punishments are just—But I say unto you, O man, whosoever doeth this the same hath great cause to repent."

Then we are reminded, "For behold, are we not all beggars? Do we not all depend upon the same Being, even God, for all the substance which we have, for both food and raiment, and for gold, and for silver, and for all the riches which we have of every kind? And behold, even at this time, ye have been calling on his name, and begging for a remission of your sins." (Mosiah 4:17–20.)

We are all "beggars," pleading for a remission of our sins. We need each other's help to repent and come unto Christ. And He needs us to help feed His sheep. All of them. He knows each one by name, and He needs our help to reach them. Lepers and Samaritans—people who are shunned—are among those for whom He has great concern.

GAINING UNDERSTANDING

I do not pretend to be an expert by writing about what friends, families, and church leaders can do to help those struggling with same-sex attraction. Rather, I discuss only what I have learned from my own experiences and those of others.

Christ has the desire, the love, and the power to gather "together the outcasts of Israel. He healeth the broken in heart, and bindeth up their wounds. He telleth the number of the stars; he calleth them all by their names. Great is our Lord, and of great power: *his understanding is infinite*." (Psalm 147:2–5; emphasis added.)

Countless news reports, magazine articles, and talk shows present an impression of who "gay" people are. But the people portrayed by the media are not the same people who silently struggle to overcome same-sex attraction and seek wholeness through Christ.

Look past the problem to the person

People who struggle with the issue of same-sex attraction have been given a great challenge; hence, we know their potential is great. Labeling them as "gay" or "lesbian" will only increase their own conviction that they truly are "homosexual" with no hope of overcoming. Help them see beyond the limits of the label and envision who they truly are: children of God with limitless, divine potential.

That is not to imply that they should deny their problem. It's important that they admit it and recognize it. The problem is real, and it is very difficult. It takes time to work through.

Seek to understand the person

It is important to seek to know the person as a unique child of God and to seek understanding of his or her unique problems. No two people are alike, even if they're struggling with the same trial. The most effective way to learn about someone is to listen attentively and nonjudgmentally. Asking sincere (not prying) questions can show that you're concerned and that you're comfortable with trying to help. The need for Christlike understanding and compassion is universal.

Seek to understand the subject

It's easy to feel overwhelmed when someone shares problems concerning same-sex attraction because so many lack knowledge of the issue. One objective of this book is to increase understanding from a gospel perspective. Other books listed in Appendix B may also be beneficial.

Some who might wish to help may have purposefully avoided the subject of homosexuality. I confided in one friend who had protected herself from the things of the world throughout her life.

She made the great sacrifice on my behalf to learn about same-sex attraction so she could assist me as I helped others and as I wrote this book. Her support and understanding have been vital.

Seek understanding of the Atonement and the power of Christ

Christ's atonement encompasses sin, weakness, trauma, and pain—anything that keeps us from reaching our potential. Assisting a person struggling with the issue of same-sex attraction can bring a deeper understanding of the Atonement.

I marvel at the power of Christ as I help others who are struggling. I see Him work in their lives, and mine, with power and might. A great spirit accompanies this work.

I never really believed in such words as *inspiration* and *promptings* until a few years ago. The Lord does give us words to say. The Spirit lets us know when and how to provide comfort, as well as when to listen and when to talk. "Neither take ye thought beforehand what ye shall say; but treasure up in your minds continually the words of life, and it shall be given you in the very hour that portion that shall be meted unto every man." (D&C 84:85.)

Not only is it important to listen to the person but it's also essential to listen to the Spirit. The guidance of the Spirit can help make up for a lack of knowledge. The Lord's understanding is infinite, and we gain the greatest understanding through Him and through the light of Christ within us. "And the light which shineth, which giveth you light, is through him who enlighteneth your eyes, which is the same light that quickeneth your understandings." (D&C 88:11.)

Seek to understand your role in the healing process

If you aren't a trained counselor, you might have certain limitations, but you can still offer assistance. Although friends I've confided in have had no experience with the subject of same-sex attraction or as counselors, they have provided great support because they've had a lifetime of experience with the Savior.

Breaking away from homosexual relationships often deluges the person with such emotions as anger, fear, rejection, denial, and rationalization. The individual may sometimes unleash emotions with little control. Try not to take it personally. Help the person focus feelings where they belong. For instance, in the case of abuse, conversing as if the offender were actually present or writing a letter that may never be sent can release the stranglehold negative feelings have had.

Emotions need to be expressed rather than squelched or minimized. At some point, traumatic events do need to be left behind—after feelings have been identified and released.

Perhaps the most difficult emotion to handle is anger, especially anger directed toward Heavenly Father, the Lord, or the Church. Strong feelings of unfairness and bitterness are common among Church members who struggle with same-sex attraction. The anger needs to be expressed, not just explained away.

There may have been misunderstanding and condemnation—maltreatment by leaders or friends within the Church. Help the person understand that the gospel is one of love and compassion, even though some people within the Church may not have been able to exemplify that.

Be willing

Helping someone through this battle takes a commitment of time and energy—spiritually, physically, and emotionally. The extent of your involvement can vary.

I love the words of Sister Chieko Okazaki: "We don't need a bishop's assignment to be kind. We don't need to sign up to be thoughtful. We don't need to be sustained by our wards to be sensitive. Rejoice in the power you have within you from Christ to be a nucleus of love, forgiveness, and compassion." ("Rejoice in Every Good Thing," *Ensign*, Nov. 1991, p. 89.)

You may be asked to sacrifice time and energy to "bear one another's burdens" and to provide emotional support as the person works through painful issues.

"And there was a certain disciple at Damascus, named Ananias; and to him said the Lord in a vision, Ananias. And he said, Behold, I am here, Lord. [I'm ready, willing, and able, even in the middle of the night.] And the Lord said unto him, Arise, and go into the street which is called Straight, and enquire in the house of Judas for one called Saul, of Tarsus: for, behold, he prayeth, and hath seen in a vision a man named Ananias coming in, and putting his hand on him, that he might receive his sight."

Now, Ananias figured Saul had some real problems and might not be worth the effort. "Then Ananias answered, Lord, I have heard by many of this man, how much evil he hath done to thy saints at Jerusalem: And here he hath authority from the chief priests to bind all that call on thy name. But the Lord said unto him, Go thy way: for he is a chosen vessel unto me, to bear my name before the Gentiles, and kings, and the children of Israel. For I will shew him how great things he must suffer for my name's sake." (Acts 9:10–16.) Could it be that many who struggle with same-sex attraction are "chosen vessels" unto the Lord.

Set limits

Know your own limits. Prayerfully consider how much time and energy you have to offer. It's just as important that you care for your own needs as it is to meet the needs of others. Set limits both for your sake and for the sake of the person struggling. Encourage him or her to open up to other people who can be trusted. Healing comes from having needs met within the bounds defined by the Lord. People, rather than just one person, help accomplish that.

Keep the confidence

It takes tremendous courage and trust to confide in others. If someone has confided in you, that is truly a sacred trust. Telling even one person could severely damage the struggling person's progress and self-esteem. Too often people have one or two others they always "trust with anything." Then each of those people "confides in" one or two other people. And so on, and so on. If that were to happen, someone could very easily leave the Church and never come back.

Confidence must be built and kept. I cannot emphasize enough how important this is.

Mostly, be a friend

Usually, once someone has disclosed his or her struggles with same-sex attraction, it's important to feel this revelation doesn't change the friendship, except to increase understanding. The person needs you to continue being a friend.

TO FAMILIES

This is a topic I cannot treat with the same degree of understanding that I have regarding the individual's struggle to overcome same-sex attraction. I suggest, particularly, reading Elder Richard G. Scott's April 1988 conference talk entitled "To Help a Loved One in Need" (*Ensign,* May 1988, pp. 60–61.) Also helpful is *Where Does a Mother Go to Resign?* by a Christian mother whose son revealed that he was "gay."

The degree of suffering of a parent often depends on the condition of the child relative to the issue. The anguish is perhaps greatest for parents who have a strong testimony of the gospel and their child reveals that he or she has decided to live a homosexual life. There can be other extreme challenges associated with this struggle, such as a child who is suicidal or suffering from AIDS. I regret that I cannot adequately address the subject of AIDS. (I've included some references concerning the subject in Appendix B.)

Your reaction to a child still living at home may differ from your reaction to a son or daughter who has already moved away. If a teenage youth reveals that he or she has homosexual feelings, listen and acknowledge that the feelings are real. Your son or daughter has already struggled with feeling different. It's important to convey unconditional love and acceptance despite your child's difficulties. Listening to how he or she is being affected can keep the lines of communication open.

If an adult son or daughter is struggling and tells you he or she is trying to overcome same-sex attraction, consider the suggestions offered in the previous section on gaining understanding and then be a friend. Ask if there is anything you can do to improve your relationship. Encouraging your child's efforts to change and reminding him or her that it's possible to change can be strengthening. If it's appropriate, help your child see how basic gospel truths apply. Try to avoid adding to the guilt he or she probably already feels.

If a son or daughter says, "I'm gay, and I've decided to live like that," the challenges are different in many ways. The following is a letter written by a mother whose son revealed he was "gay:"

When Kevin returned from his mission, he flew to Provo to continue his college life. He was excited about being on the BYU campus for the first time. He was also going to become reacquainted with his sister who was a student there.

Three weeks later they called to tell me they would be commuting to school from the Salt Lake area. I insisted the decision was stupid and wanted to know the real reason for it. My daughter called back the next morning, and for the first time in my life I heard the words, "Kevin is gay." I didn't cry because, honestly, the Spirit whispered the words to me before she did. I was frozen.

Kevin had agreed to let her tell me because he was at the end of the road. He had prayed for twenty-one years and had lost all hope. We are a very close family, and I was told later that if we had rejected him at that moment, he would have ended his life. But the Spirit was with me, saying words, allowing me to make the right sounds.

When Kevin and I spoke, he wept, and all those years of denial, self-accusations, and disbelief came tumbling out, all in bitter, heart-wrenching sobs.

I told his father for him. His father's reaction was "Come home for a semester, come and talk, come for hugs, come for a blessing, come and we'll cry."

They planned a week's vacation together, Kevin, his father, and his younger brothers. At first they tiptoed, and then they found the strength to sit and talk. But they did not approach the subject. That was too hard.

Kevin went to Social Services because we asked him to. He was told from the first moment he could successfully change through therapy. We were so excited, and he was so petrified! After twenty-one years of denial, he wanted to explore and find out who he really was. We wanted him back the way we thought he used to be.

Four months of therapy brought a trust in his therapist but a deep depression and a self-esteem that visibly shrank every day. And so, in January, he went back to Utah to do whatever he desired.

My emotions ranged from total despair to metallic fear to joy that he still had a testimony and still loved his Father in Heaven to anger—lots of anger with guilt poured all over the top. Anger that such a wonderful, loving person could be afflicted with such an existence. Anger that God would not answer such sincere, pain-wracked prayers from such an innocent boy. Anger at a church where I am afraid even to whisper "Kevin is gay" lest he be totally ostracized. Anger at a church that has no place for such a talented, spiritual person.

And fear when I found out he had been raped and was searching for answers in gay bars and had only homosexual friends and was not living the commandments, which he knows are essential for eternal life.

And gratitude for a bishop who knows his name and lovingly chastises him if too much time lapses in his church attendance, and gratitude for home teachers who bring cookies and their sweet spirit into his life.

I still hold my breath. I've lost the anger at my Father in Heaven as I remember that my thoughts are not His thoughts and my ways are not His ways. But I get angry at those Church members who group all homosexuals under one label. Each one is an individual, each one a separate story.

Last month, for the first time in a long time, I felt hope. Kevin said, "I found an apartment so I can live alone, and one day, Mom, I will walk away and leave this life because it means nothing to me." I hope we live that long. But if it never comes to pass, I have learned the meaning of unconditional love for Kevin and for my Father in Heaven.

The pain, anger, confusion, and doubt are often as intense for the family as they are for the person who has homosexual desires. Some parents may suffer less than their child does, and others may suffer more. Thus, everyone involved needs to be patient and understanding of each other's struggles.

Here are some suggestions that may help family members deal with this difficult situation.

Avoid blaming yourself

A child's homosexual desires are not the family's fault. Blaming yourself only damages your own spiritual and emotional well-being.

Some parents blame spouses or leaders because of their strong desire to find the cause or the solution for their child's homosexual feelings. Although difficulties in the home may have contributed to your child's feelings, it is no longer believed that families *cause* same-sex attraction. The cause is most likely a complicated combination of factors that are still only partially understood.

Parents can end up suffering and regretting every tiny, human mistake they ever made while parenting if they blame themselves for their child's problems. By our very nature, imperfect humans are parents—and children—to other imperfect humans here on earth. The Savior can compensate for any errors made by earthly parents as long as we look to Him. It is part of the plan.

The struggle isn't necessarily related to anything the parent has actually done. One important factor is the child's perception of how he or she was treated in the home, not the actual treatment. There may be things you did during your child's growing up that you regret. You may wish to ask forgiveness for those and for whatever pain those actions may have caused. Even though your child may not have chosen the feelings that led him or her into same-sex attraction, your child alone must accept responsibility for the actions he or she has taken because of those feelings.

President Spencer W. Kimball said, "Righteous parents who strive to develop wholesome influences for their children will be held blameless at the last day." ("Ocean Currents and Family Influences," *Ensign,* Nov. 1974, p. 111.)

Avoid blaming yourself

I realize I just said this, but it's such an important point and such a widespread, destructive problem, it seemed to bear repeating.

Try to respond compassionately

Compassion will help you avoid saying or thinking, "How could you do this to us? How could you do this to yourself? You know it's a horrible sin!"

Ask yourself, "What can I do to help my son or daughter fight the battle of a lifetime? A battle so difficult that the worst of it goes on for months or even years, often producing suicidal thoughts." It's easy to fall into the trap of thinking that it is a simple matter of choice. It is true that nothing is more important than eternal salvation. But I bear witness it is not that simple.

I didn't care about eternal salvation during the worst of it. I wanted to live through the day. I wanted love and acceptance. I wasn't always completely clear on right and wrong. Satan kept erasing the lines. I did have the agency to choose, but that ability had been weakened by past experiences and situations. At times, I went with the only option that seemed livable for the moment, not for the eternities.

Those who have gone so far as to leave or ignore the Church in choosing a homosexual life may feel they have finally found self-acceptance, which can be deeply comforting after years of self-condemnation. It can be difficult for them to choose to be miserable again while they work through the issue.

Seek to provide unconditional love

Your child probably already knows how you feel about homosexual relationships because of your testimony of the gospel. Concentrate on what you know from your own experiences. Bear witness of the Savior in word and deed. Strive to love as He would love—unconditionally. Seek to follow Christ's example in rejecting the sin but loving the sinner.

Elder Richard G. Scott says, "Love without limitations. When in a dream Lehi partook of the fruit of the tree of life and was filled with joy, his first thought was to share it with each member of his family, including the disobedient." ("To Help a Loved One in Need," *Ensign*, May 1988, p. 60.)

As you attempt to build or rebuild the relationship, try to separate love and support from rescuing. Parents sometimes try to "save the injured child." The child must go through his or her own healing process to grow through this trial.

Certainly, the situation becomes more complicated when a son or daughter becomes belligerent, disrupting the peace and spirit of the home. For instance, the child might insist on bringing home the person with whom he or she is involved. Prayerfully decide how much distance you feel is needed to set and maintain limits.

Care for your own needs

Taking time to do the things that will preserve your own spiritual and emotional health is vital. You will most likely experience all of the elements of grief, including anger, denial, rejection, sorrow, and, finally, acceptance. Seeking comfort by expressing feelings is just as important for you as it is for your child. Unfortunately, because of the stigmas attached to having homosexual desires, especially in the Church, your first inclination might be to keep it a secret. Ask your child's permission, and carefully consider those with whom you can share your burden. If your child does not want anyone to know, it's important to respect those wishes. Letting people know can make it more difficult for your son or daughter to find acceptance.

You may want to seek help from a counselor or a bishop, particularly if your child requests confidentiality. Find a counselor who shares your values and convictions. Be aware that many counselors may believe you should simply accept the "fact" that your son or daughter is "gay" and there is no possibility of change. It might turn out that your child does spend the rest of his or her life in homosexual relationships, but hold to your belief that it's possible to do otherwise.

Some parents have been strengthened by becoming educated on the subject. Helping to support others struggling with same-sex attraction has assisted in the healing process.

Hold firmly to the iron rod

Christ provides the greatest comfort and understanding that can be found; thus, it is especially important to hold firmly to gospel principles. Unfortunately, some Latter-day Saint family members with a loved one involved in a homosexual relationship may believe that the loved one has no choice. It's easy to understand. They witness the intense struggle firsthand and become convinced that anything other than a homosexual life for their child or sibling is impossible. Parents, like their children, may begin to question Church leadership and modern-day prophets.

Some parents may even believe they have received personal revelation concerning the correctness of homosexual behavior. Satan, the great imitator, subtly distorts and reshapes intellectual reasoning, along with such emotions as anger, doubt, and protectiveness of a child. In this way, he can draw the parent away from the truthfulness of the gospel. The situation is often worsened if the child has been treated unfairly or harshly by a Church leader. Occasionally, parents also encounter Church members who don't know how to react, or who react negatively to them as parents of a child with same-sex attraction.

Our Savior wants us to find happiness not in the moment, through "earthly" means, but to overcome sin and gain eternal life because that brings the only true and lasting joy. Continue to pray and hope for your child's safe return from life outside of the Lord's boundaries. It is important not to lose faith in the gospel. Jesus Christ is the greatest source of strength.

Enlist the help of the One who can help the most

After you've done all you can to repair or build the relationship with your child, hand it over to the Lord. Constant worry destroys faith. They are opposites. Fasting and prayer enlist the powers of heaven.

Neither you nor the Lord can interfere with your child's agency. Do what you can, and have faith the Lord will take care of the rest. "For we know that it is by grace that we are saved, after all we can do." (2 Nephi 25:23.)

TO SPOUSES

Just as I do not fully understand what the parent of someone struggling with same-sex attraction experiences, I do not fully understand the trials of a person whose spouse struggles with homosexual feelings. I've spoken with those in this difficult situation. I've heard the pain in their questions and comments. I've seen considerable innocent suffering.

The former wife of a man who is now living a homosexual life agreed to let me share her story:

> One of my greatest dreams in life was to have children, but I found myself married to a man who was gay and refused to have sex with me. It is really hard to explain ALL of the effects the marriage had on me. Venturing into that locked area (my heart) opens up the flood gates of pain and grief and anger and unrelenting questions. My prayers for understanding or solutions seem to go unheeded.
>
> Certainly, one of the toughest parts of the whole ordeal was the aloneness. When Lance divulged his homosexuality to me, he begged me to keep it confidential. We both knew how damaging that information would be to relationships with family and friends. We knew of their prejudices, their harsh judgments, and that they might ultimately disown or shun us both—him for being gay and me for being married to him. We also knew that it would put his career in jeopardy. So we had to make sure that we didn't allow even a hint of suspicion.
>
> We spent many nights crying and talking and sobbing and praying about "his trial." Lance said repeatedly that God had played a "cruel joke" on him. One time I suggested that the "cruel joke" was on both of us. He seemed genuinely shocked that I felt included in the suffering. He honestly had no clue how devastating it was to be married to a man who was gay. Perhaps he thought my pain was insignificant compared to his. Lance was too focused on his own trial to see mine. I wasn't even sure the Lord listened or cared much.
>
> The isolation was compounded daily. I died inside when I heard gay jokes being told, but couldn't let that show. Friends who were getting married came to ask advice about sex. I just made things up that sounded feasible and sensitive and like I was the happiest woman alive.
>
> Everyone around me knew that I wanted children and had hoped to start a family right away. I was barraged with questions from family, friends, ward members, and business associates. Each time someone asked if I was pregnant, I felt a stinging

knife go through my heart. I finally decided to tell people that we "were unable to have children." At least they were empathetic to that and quit asking.

My dream of having children was totally blocked and not only could I not grieve, I had to pretend that I was happy and hopeful. I loved Lance deeply. I knew the depth of his pain and his struggle, and I didn't want to add to that by letting him see how badly I ached about being childless. So I had yet one more pain to hide.

Sometimes I hated Lance. I hated him for using me as a "cover." I hated him for not overcoming his sexual preference. I hated him for all the pain he caused me that I had to deal with alone. I hated him for not even trying to have sex so that we could at least have children. I hated him for not seeing that I had needs too and that the world didn't revolve around his homo-sexuality. I hated him for letting his homosexuality ruin our relationship and for placing his sexual preference above the love we had developed.

Then I would feel guilty for hating him for something he believed was inherent in who he was. He believed he had no choice in being gay, and he believed it was impossible to change.

It was devastating to be married to a man who wouldn't touch me. My own normal sexual feelings didn't cease; they just became frustrated beyond belief. I slept next to a man that I was married to, was passionately in love with, and I remained a vir-gin. It was hard to hold on to self-esteem when that occurred. I ached constantly. I felt like a failure as a person, as a wife. I tried to convince myself that sex was unnecessary in a good relation-ship. Whether or not that is true, it wasn't the issue.

The issue was that my husband would rather have sex with another man (something I found repulsive) than have sex with me (something he found repulsive). It's tough trying to emerge from that without feeling lower than the most repulsive animal on earth. I could not fathom that my husband would risk so much to have sex with another man while his willing wife remained untouched.

I remember one night I sobbed so hard that I began vomiting. The ordeal went on for hours—sobbing, retching. Finally, I collapsed on the tile floor of the bathroom where I spent the longest night of my entire life. Apparently I had gotten married alone—I was the only one who had made a commitment that day to build a marriage. Lance said that all he did on our wedding day was build a lie and get stuck living it.

He progressively became cold, distant, detached, angry. He slept on the couch. He winced if I came too close. The anger he had was directed at me—as though my mere existence was the cause of his misery. He acted like he hated me just because I was a woman. Or because I wasn't a man.

My faith got lost somewhere. Lance didn't choose to be gay. I don't think anyone who is homosexual chooses to be gay. To what advantage? Lance tried to fight it, deny it, cover it, hide it, and plead with the Lord to take it away from him. He went to his bishop for help and was counseled to get married and read the scriptures and the homosexual feelings would go away. He followed the counsel, and the feelings didn't go away. They grew more intense.

The tug of war between the Church's stand and the grueling reality became too great. We divorced several years ago. Lance left the Church because he felt he was being condemned for being the way God created him. I watched him ask for answers, go for counseling, pray, plead, struggle. I heard no solutions, no ways to truly change, only counsel to deny his feelings and live that lie—it didn't work. It nearly destroyed both of us. I lost my best friend, my husband, my dreams of having children, my confidence, and a big chunk of my faith because the man I fell in love with was gay, and nobody seemed to know how to fix that.

The spouse of one who struggles with homosexual desires often faces pain and conflict just as deep as that of their husband or wife. I don't know why we are given the trials we're given. I do know that just as each trial brings the possibility of destruction, it also brings the opportunity for triumph. Just as a spouse's struggle with same-sex attraction can destroy a marriage, so it can also build an eternal one—creating a depth of understanding and love few marriages attain.

A spouse who does not seek change

When a husband or wife reveals same-sex attraction and is unrepentant, you are faced with some very difficult issues. The avalanche of emotions often include an overwhelming sense of betrayal, self-blame, deep despair, feelings of inadequacy, a loss of self-esteem, and, with a husband who is sexually involved in the lifestyle, the fear of AIDS. Some spouses may deny that there's a problem and try to ignore it. As a result, the marriage suffers greatly and the possibility of healing diminishes.

It is very common for spouses of those struggling with homosexual desires to believe that they are somehow at fault. That is not so. Sometimes those struggling will even lash out in frustration and blame the wife or husband, claiming they have been forced to turn to same-sex relationships because of a lack of understanding by their spouse. The problem did not originate with you, and your spouse's problem doesn't mean something is wrong with you. If you have been led to believe that your having been a better husband or wife would have prevented it, please understand, that is not true.

Your spouse's decision to continue sinning in a homosexual manner can affect your eternal progress. "Be ye not unequally yoked together with unbelievers: for what fellowship hath righteousness with unrighteousness? and what communion hath light with darkness?" (2 Corinthians 6:14.)

A spouse may try to convince you that it is "just the way I am" and ask for an arrangement in the marriage that allows involvement in other relationships because the behavior "can't be helped." The truth is, the behavior can be overcome if he or she is willing to make the tremendous effort required. If your spouse chooses not to put forth the effort, seek guidance from an understanding bishop, stake president, and/or a counselor to prayerfully decide what should be done.

A spouse who is struggling to overcome

Even when a spouse is repentant and seeks freedom from same-sex attraction, the road is extremely difficult for everyone involved.

As stated previously, self-blame is a common reaction. Keep in mind that you are not to blame for your spouse's struggle, even if accusations are made to that effect. The problem likely began long before the two of you met.

To provide support for their spouse, some married people neglect or minimize their own pain and suffering. Acknowledging and expressing your feelings is an important part of gaining the strength to handle the difficult situation. You will likely encounter feelings of betrayal, neglect, deep hurt, and abandonment. You will also likely lose interest in pursuing an intimate relationship with someone who has recently been sexually involved outside of the marriage. And there is also the reality of AIDS to consider.

Carefully guard your spiritual, emotional, and physical health. It can be difficult to find a balance between helping a spouse find freedom from same-sex attraction and meeting your own needs. Your struggles may well be just as burdensome, and you have every right to seek understanding and patience. Counselors, inspired Church leaders, and friends can offer support. Prayerfully consider which ones would be helpful and would keep the confidence.

If your spouse is not able to resist temptation immediately, set limits. It may be necessary to ask yourself such questions as "Am I willing to continue in such a marriage?" "Is my spouse honestly working towards gaining freedom from homosexual relationships?" If your spouse has been sexually active outside of the marriage, take precautions against the risk of sexually transmitted diseases.

The companionship of the Spirit is essential. Personal needs and desires can get in the way of personal revelation. Pray to know through the Spirit what should be done.

One woman whose husband gained freedom from compelling homosexual desires stated, "I spent lots of time in the temple. It helped me keep an eternal perspective on all of this. I focused my time and energy on keeping the family, children, and the household functioning. I told myself that my husband was in charge of his healing. I prayed for him daily, but also took care of myself and the rest of the family. At some points during his healing, I honestly felt greater spiritual growth than I've ever experienced."

TO LEADERS

I can say, without a doubt, that my bishop had more influence on my returning to the Church and continuing to seek the Spirit than any other one person. I looked forward to my visits with Bishop Garey, much as a homeless person looks forward to the opening of the soup kitchen. I was spiritually starving, and the bishop provided nourishment. He was strict the few times he needed to be and always showed an outpouring of love afterwards. His love provided the power and motivation for me to continue trying.

On the other hand, I know a number of people who have never gone back to church because of how they were treated by their bishops. I am not saying they are justified in their decision, but I do know that an understanding, patient Church leader is essential in helping a person find freedom from same-sex attraction.

It is my hope that although I lack the knowledge and experience of a Church leader, my experiences with my bishop can prove helpful. This section describes several ways in which Bishop Garey assisted me in my struggle to overcome. Some of the suggestions are in the Church's pamphlet *Understanding and Helping Those Who Have Homosexual Problems.*

Convey compassion and acceptance

My bishop responded with compassion and concern. When I first started seeing him, I was unable to feel the Spirit at church. No one there knew of my struggles, and I feared condemnation.

Even if there is no rejection, the threat of it can be intense. The fear of the loss of Church membership and lack of understanding can keep people from confiding in their bishop.

Bishop Garey came to know everything I had done, yet he accepted and loved me anyway. He did whatever it took to bring the Spirit into our sessions together. I often hated to leave because I knew I would feel terribly alone again.

Genuine Christlike love is such a powerful source of healing. People in the early stages of overcoming homosexual desires are seldom able to feel that love directly from heaven, and you can serve as a "well of living water" to provide nourishment. You can help them to feel accepted by a Church whose members may have left them feeling rejected. It is important that they come to accept themselves not as "homosexuals" but as disciples of Christ who are struggling with a difficult trial.

Offer time and attention

I know bishops have a million responsibilities. Somehow my bishop always found time for me. I met with him every week or so for nearly three years. I suppose that seems like a lot of time, but somehow he knew it was necessary. So did I. He gave me his home phone number and told me I could call whenever I needed to. I seldom called him at home but greatly appreciated knowing that I could.

He'd call me if I didn't show up at church meetings and ask if I was all right. His phone calls helped me attend the following week, even at times when I'd decided to stop.

Be open to inspiration

Common sense alone does not suffice. No Church disciplinary council was ever held for me, even when I suggested it. I'm not saying my bishop's response would be appropriate in every case: "I feel compelled to tell you that you're working your way straight to hell." In fact, a few months later when I spoke of that, he found it impossible to believe he'd ever said it. "You must be kidding. A bishop would never say that to someone." Well, a bishop who was filled with the Spirit did. The Spirit knew what I needed and when I needed it.

The Church's booklet on helping those with homosexual problems can be a valuable tool in counseling and making decisions. Of course, the decision whether or not to hold a disciplinary council needs to be an inspired one because each individual struggle is different.

I slipped up several times, many months after I first went in to see the bishop. For a while I could not find the strength I needed to avoid Tracy. I know my bishop was guided by the Spirit not to take

Church action. I could tell he was about to say, "That's it!" Then the Spirit would instruct him to do otherwise.

Homosexual behavior is often addictive behavior, sexually and/or emotionally, and is more similar to alcoholism in its addictive nature than it is to typical heterosexual infidelity. Frequently there will have been a history of abuse, and other issues are likely to be involved—a confusion of identity, a conviction that there is no hope of finding freedom and happiness, and anger towards God and "church authority," to name a few. Just because a person cannot alter behavior right away doesn't necessarily mean his or her best effort isn't being put forth. Yet others may be trying to get away with whatever they can. A spouse and all those who are trying to help will need to exercise great caution in the way they encourage the person who is struggling with same-sex attraction. Some depressed people may already be suicidal, and pushing too hard could push them over the edge. Your power of discernment is vital.

Build confidence

Low self-esteem is common among those who struggle with homosexual desires. I had no self-esteem at the beginning of the battle, and Bishop Garey helped me feel like a choice daughter of a loving Heavenly Father. He always had something positive to say, even when I made mistakes. I came to believe that maybe Heavenly Father really did think I was worthwhile because the man He had sent as judge in His place was conveying just that.

You may want to select a single positive action that the person is capable of doing, an action which, if done consistently, will strengthen the person spiritually and emotionally. For example, you could challenge the person to read the scriptures each day. It is often easier to start a positive behavior than to stop a negative one. Acknowledging his or her effort can enhance the person's self-esteem and desire to continue trying.

Personal responsibility to overcome should be emphasized, but it also helps to hear acknowledgment of the difficulty of the challenge. My bishop reinforced and genuinely complimented my progress at every stage. He helped me establish a sense of self-worth and trust.

The relationship between the person who struggles with this issue and Heavenly Father can be improved through your kindness and example. There is often anger and mistrust directed towards Heavenly Father, and the person's perceptions of you can reshape perceptions of Him.

Discuss the details of homosexual behavior sensitively

Confessing homosexual activity may well be even more difficult and embarrassing than confessing illicit heterosexual activity. It is important to be sensitive to that. I know people who have been humiliated because their bishops asked for intimate details of their sexual involvement. Asking for such explicit details is unnecessary.

To assess the seriousness of the sins, perhaps you'll need to ask about the frequency of sex, fantasizing, masturbation and/or pornography; yet inquiring about intimate and unnecessary details can still be avoided. The bishop's handbook suggests you ask "questions that will help you understand the person's feelings and intentions as well as the nature and seriousness of the problem. For example, you could ask: 'What difficulties are you having? How long have they existed? How deeply involved are you in homosexual thoughts, feelings, or behavior? What effect are these problems having in your life? What do you think can be done to improve the situation?'" (*Understanding and Helping Those Who Have Homosexual Problems* [Salt Lake City: The Church of Jesus Christ of Latter-day Saints, 1992], p. 3.)

Just because a person hasn't been sexually involved for quite some time, even years, doesn't mean the problem has necessarily been solved. Ask if he or she still battles thoughts. Does the individual believe he or she is homosexual? Regardless of outward behavior, there still might be inward struggles with which the individual needs help.

Be aware that some men and women struggling with homosexual desires might have problems interacting with men who occupy positions of authority. Those who seek counsel will need to feel they are being understood and cared for, rather than controlled or dominated.

Some of the women who struggle harbor ill feelings towards men because of previous abuse. Talking with any man about sexual situations or other private matters can be extremely difficult for them. Such conversation can set off feelings they experienced when they were being abused or violated. Sensitivity is essential.

Find others who can help

Prayerfully recommend a professional counselor, one who is professionally and spiritually equipped to assist. Work closely with the counselor to discuss ways of helping the individual. I strongly believe the counselor should be a faithful Church member. Other therapists may believe a "homosexual is a homosexual" and no one should attempt to change. Also, the presence of the Spirit in counseling is a great asset.

Healing can be accelerated through positive relationships with other Church members who are compassionate and supportive. If no one else has been told, encourage the person to do so. Honoring trust is especially important, however. No one else should be told until you've received express permission to share the confidence. Be aware of the difficulty and the fear the person might have of telling others. He or she has probably already struggled with acceptance and cannot afford to feel any more rejection at church.

Assigning faithful home teachers and visiting teachers is another effective means of helping. You know the situation as well as most of the ward members. Who is dedicated to the gospel and living its teachings fully? Who is nonjudgmental? Who can be trusted? Who is willing to devote the time necessary to help? Once you've assigned people, encourage openness, honesty, and trust within those rela-tionships. Home teachers and visiting teachers who fulfill their callings can be instrumental in helping. You may want to evaluate the effectiveness of the relationship periodically and make new assignments if necessary.

Heterosexual relationships are not a "cure" for same-sex attraction

A long-range goal of working with a Church member struggling with same-sex attraction may be an affectionate relationship with a member of the opposite sex. But those attractions cannot be forced.

A heterosexual relationship is not the solution; it is the result of progress towards that solution.

Encouraging the individual who is struggling with same-sex attraction to date members of the opposite sex before he or she is ready can inhibit growth and change. It takes a great deal of time to work through difficult issues concerning homosexual desires and progress to the point where problems with attractions toward the opposite sex can be addressed.

Again, as President Hinckley stated, "Marriage should not be viewed as a therapeutic step to solve problems such as homosexual inclinations." ("Reverence and Morality," *Ensign*, May 1987, p. 47.)

Learn from them

The best way to learn about the problems of the individual struggling with same-sex attraction is to listen to his or her problems with the guidance of the Spirit. No two situations are the same.

Most people will appreciate the opportunity to discuss their struggles with someone who is strong in the Church and from whom they do not fear rejection. They may not have had the chance to do that before.

Listening to the individual and the Spirit are the two most powerful ways you can receive the guidance needed to invite people back to the Savior.

MY HOPES FOR THE FUTURE

Our most effective work in helping people overcome same-sex attraction will be done with the youth. Few have made a habit of sexually acting out at that point, and it is during the early years that we can effectively move to prevent the destructive forces of low self-esteem and lack of acceptance.

We need to do more than simply tell our youth that homosexual behavior is sinful because that simply is not enough. The struggle with homosexual desires contributes to the individual's feelings of self-hatred. Many righteous, stalwart young people have become confused when they have found their feelings to be in conflict with their beliefs. They need to understand the difference between feelings and behavior. They need to be able to separate themselves from the identity the world is handing them—"Hey kid, accept it. You're gay."

Perhaps we fear that talking about a problem will create a problem. Young people hear about homosexual behavior from their peers and the media no matter how we try to protect them. Unfortunately, most information they get on the subject is the world's view.

I believe we should all strive to avoid being judgmental or prejudiced. I also believe we need to be judicious when it comes to what our children are taught in school. We need to teach our youth at home and church that yes, homosexual behavior is sin, but if they have those desires, there is help. Then we must provide that help.

The youth who struggle with this issue need to understand they are loved and accepted. Much is required of them, but that's because they have been given much, not because they have somehow been short-changed.

We need to teach Christlike love, rather than judging or making fun of others. Youth may continue to do that, but they learn from our examples.

Relief Society presidents can often be an invaluable resource to women in their wards or branches who have suffered abuse from men, including women who struggle with same-sex attraction and others who do not. Some may not feel comfortable talking with men. For instance, one woman I know was sexually molested many times by her father while she was growing up, including once the night before he baptized her. Asking a person who has had that kind of experience to trust a man, even a "priesthood authority," before she has worked through some of her problems, may be asking her to do the impossible. Relief Society presidents who demonstrate empathy and compassion can establish a "safe" setting for a woman who is struggling with sensitive issues and trying to gather strength to counsel with priesthood leaders. In this role, Relief Society presidents are, of course, obligated to maintain confidences, just as bishops do. (All Church members need to constantly guard against disclosing confidential matters they become aware of.)

Some members of the Church may think there are too few in the Church who struggle with same-sex attraction to warrant concern. Estimates vary widely, but the percentage of Church members who have this proclivity is probably the same as it is for the general population, though there are likely fewer in the Church who have acted on their same-sex attraction.

Christ is concerned with the one, and there is more than one person who has this trial. People who struggle with this issue are in Relief Society and priesthood quorums and in our Young Men and Young Women programs. They usually look and act like everyone else. They're battling desperately to fit in—to avoid feeling different—and many are losing the battle.

No matter what the struggle or trial, we need to join together as Christians to bring individuals into the fold.

There are people wandering around lost in the same dark, bitter cold storm I was in. It's desolate, and the only sign of comfort they can find is forbidden by the Lord. They need somewhere else to go—a place of warmth, a haven of peace.

May we follow President Spencer W. Kimball's admonition: "I hope that if any of God's children are out in spiritual darkness, you will come to them with a lamp and light their way; if they are out in the cold of spiritual bleakness with its frigidity penetrating their bones, you will come to them holding their hands a little way, you will walk miles and miles with them lifting them, strengthening them, encouraging them and inspiring them." Amen. ("What I Hope You Will Teach My Grandchildren," 1966 address to seminary and institute teachers, quoted in Vaughn J. Featherstone, *Charity Never Faileth* [Salt Lake City: Deseret Book Co., 1980], p. 56.)

Afterword

Soon after I finished writing the manuscript that has become this book, my relationship with the man I was dating began to flourish. We were recently married in the temple for time and all eternity.

I wish to say to those who are hoping eternal marriage is possible, that it is possible. And you do not have to try and "make do" with someone. For years I had thought that getting married was something I would have to do just to satisfy heaven's requirement and to put myself in line for eternal life. However, to my ongoing amazement, marriage has been a tremendous blessing. I have found in our relationship more expression of feelings and emotions than in any other I have known, and to a greater extent than I had hoped on even my most optimistic days.

No other experience I have had compares to that which my husband and I shared when we knelt across the altar, listening to the words of the sealer and feeling the Spirit bear witness of those words. The moment echoed and reverberated with promises of kingdoms, principalities, and eternal life in the presence of God.

To those who currently view the possibility of a temple marriage with apathy, disdain, or despair, I testify that you can find peace and fulfillment in this life through a relationship with Jesus Christ. I found those blessings before I found my husband. I never knew whether or not I would get married in this life. I did know I would have to give up homosexual relationships and do all I could to prepare for eternal life.

I was happy single. I'm happy married. I left the fact that I am now married out of the main body of this book because marriage was never intended to be the focus. I wanted the real-life ending to remain as it was: the maiden was rescued by the Prince of Peace and lived happily ever after.

Appendix A

David

For most of my life I struggled with homosexual attractions. I was molested by my grandfather at age four and first exposed to pornography at seven. By age ten I was sexually acting out with neighborhood boys. At eleven, I had my first homosexual experience with an adult. I enjoyed the contact and attention those activities gave me and was soon addicted. At age fifteen, I had two homosexual experiences with the organist at my church, and he introduced me to alcohol.

I was soon smoking pot and beginning to use drugs to escape the reality that what the kids were saying was true: that I was a "sissy," a "fag," a "queer," a "homosexual." I don't think they knew of my activity, but because I had difficulty relating with the "male" role, I tended to walk, talk, and in many ways act differently than other boys. I absolutely hated this ostracism and name-calling. I would have given anything to be liked and accepted by them. I did get along with the girls and enjoyed their company and friendship, but as I grew older, I found that I was not attracted to them physically like the other boys were.

I kept hoping and waiting for the day when I would grow up and be attracted to girls. It never happened. As I entered high school, my homosexual activity began to diminish because I could not handle the guilt of influencing others. So, for the most part, I resorted to pornography, masturbation, and homosexual fantasizing. I continued to escape reality by abusing drugs.

My teachers liked me, and I was an honor student. I rarely gave my parents trouble. I hungered for attention and approval of others and developed many talents and abilities in an attempt to gain this approval. The pull between bad and good was ripping me apart. I could not continue going on that way. I did not ask for or want to be the "sexual freak" I had become.

If there really was a God, how could he allow this to happen to me?

It seemed as if I had two options and continuing to live this double life was not one of them. I could "come out of the closet" and move to Hollywood or San Francisco where I could indulge in that which came naturally to me, or I could commit suicide. By the time I graduated from high school, I hated my condition, myself, and my life. At this all-time low, the Lord began to work a miracle and prepare me to accept the gospel of Jesus Christ.

I had many Mormon friends from high school who had tried to share their beliefs with me. They began inviting me to their activities. When I was with them, I felt a special spirit. That feeling was something I had never experienced, something I wanted and needed.

One day I asked a close friend what the Church meant to him, and he said: "The gospel is the most important thing in my life." The Spirit hit me with great force, and I knew what he said was true. I began taking the missionary lessons. For the first time, life took on meaning. Heavenly Father loved me and wanted me to straighten my life out, so I could return to Him someday. I was soon baptized.

It was a great blessing to have a second chance in life and have all of the sins of my past washed away. I soon found, though, that the homosexual attractions were not washed away with everything else. At first it was very hard on me, but I decided that it did not matter what temptations I had, just as long as I did not act on them. So I continued keeping myself strong and free from homosexual activity.

President Kimball had said that every worthy young man should serve a mission. I felt worthy and desired to follow the prophet's counsel. Papers filled out, physicals passed, hair cut short, pictures taken, and bishop's interview completed, I went in for my interview with the stake president. His best friend's son had just been sent home from his mission because of homosexual activity. After hearing my story, my stake president felt it would be best if I served a stake mission instead, and possibly a full-time mission, later.

I enjoyed serving and did so faithfully. But at the same time, people began asking why I had not gone on a full-time mission. Can you imagine trying to explain that one? I began to doubt myself and question my place in the Church. If I truly had been forgiven of my past transgressions, then why had I not been allowed to go on a full-time mission? Maybe repentance was for everyone but the "homosexual." I wondered how my stake president could do this terrible thing to me. I became very frustrated and discouraged. My self-esteem and spirituality took a real dive.

I worked hard and managed to save my testimony. I started dating a Mormon girl, Barbara, and we hit it off great. I began to think about marriage and decided to tell her of my past struggles. She handled it quite well. Eventually, I asked her to marry me, and she said yes. We were married in the temple. Although I did not get baptized or married to cure my homosexual orientation, I hoped those things might help. I soon realized after we were married that the homosexual attractions were still present.

I again fell to the temptation of masturbation and fantasizing during the years of our marriage that followed. These occurrences left me very unhappy, and I suffered spiritually. Then, one night our baby needed a blessing due to her chemotherapy, and I felt unworthy to give it. How could I do this to her, my other children, my wife, and myself? I lay in bed and wept in my wife's arms because of this experience. At that moment, something happened deep within me. I was finally ready to do whatever it might take to be free of the condition that kept interfering with my life and happiness.

We sought counsel from a therapist who helped me see the valuable person I really was and who boosted my self-esteem. Things began to change for the better. He reaffirmed the fact that it doesn't matter what our temptations are as long as we don't act on them or entertain them in our minds.

I'd seen miracles in my life and wondered why the Lord could not perform another one by granting me my righteous desires. I feel the Lord heard my prayers and led me to others and worked in many ways to bring about my healing. The miracles occurred gradually.

Although I had not been acting out and was usually worthy to hold a temple recommend, I still felt that my spirituality was being blocked. I now feel that my healing has removed that block as I have witnessed the companionship and promptings of the Spirit in ways I never dreamed possible. Today, I am free of the struggles of trying to resist homosexual temptation. The envy, lust, infatuation and fantasizing which were constant, are now gone. The chains by which Satan had me bound have been broken, and I am finally free.

The relationship with my wife has greatly improved emotionally, spiritually, and sexually. I am attracted to her and enjoy being intimate with her.

The Lord has taken my trials and weaknesses and turned them into strengths. I am thankful for the talents, abilities, compassion, and understanding for others, as well as for the strong testimony and understanding of the gospel that have come by working through my problems. "And if men come unto me I will show unto them their weakness. I give unto men weakness that they may be humble; and my grace is sufficient for all men that humble themselves before me; for if they humble themselves before me, and have faith in me, then will I make weak things become strong unto them." (Ether 12:27.)

Really understanding same-sex attraction and why I had those desires seemed to de-sexualize them. Several Christian books and other resources helped. Learning about same-sex attraction from this new perspective was like hearing the gospel for the first time. Things began to click and finally make sense. I knew what I read and heard was true.

I would like to share how Barbara and I got through a time in our lives when we were faced with an overwhelming situation. It isn't about homosexual desires, but I think it is applicable. When our daughter was diagnosed with cancer, Barbara and I were having a very hard time handling it. We spent days sobbing in each other's arms. Finally, we realized that in order to get through the ordeal, we were going to have to put it in the Lord's hands, and prayed: "Heavenly Father, you know how much we love and want to keep our precious daughter, but we have faith in thy will and know if you want her back now, that is what is best, and we are willing to let you take her." I can't adequately describe the peace and comfort we received because of that prayer. We were fine from then on and did well through all of the treatments and trials we endured thereafter with our daughter. I am happy to say that she has been in remission for five years and we feel very good about her staying with us for a long time. I have learned to do all I can do and then put the rest in the Lord's hands.

"Come unto me, all ye that labour and are heavy laden, and I will give you rest. Take my yoke upon you, and learn of me; for I am meek and lowly in heart: and ye shall find rest unto your souls. For my yoke is easy, and my burden is light." (Matthew 11:28-30.) I know that if we will do this, no matter what our trials are, we will be blessed and find that, indeed, with God nothing is impossible.

JEFF

I grew up a very shy, introverted kid, a loner for the most part. I felt terribly insecure and inadequate around guys my own age or older and avoided them as much as possible.

My dad wasn't home very often, so I did not have a role model. My parents never displayed any verbal or physical affection. I interpreted their inability to express love as meaning that I must not be lovable, that something must be dreadfully wrong with me. Added to this were a lot of hurt feelings caused by my dad. Whenever I'd cry, he'd tell me to "stop acting like a woman," which only added to my feelings of inadequacy.

As a young boy, I became aware of my physical attraction to other boys. I now see that all I really wanted was to belong and have some male friends, to feel normal, rather than be a "sissy." But all I could do was admire other boys from the sidelines.

One day, I had played "doctor" with a boy I was friends with—the normal exploration that can happen among children. The kids at school started saying that we'd had sex together and soon it seemed like that was all anyone at school was talking about. It was absolutely the most humiliating experience of my life, and from that point on, I reverted to being a loner. I became consumed with my attraction toward guys.

There were even worse problems at home. It was obvious that my parents weren't in love with each other, that they were just playing the role of a married couple for the sake of their children. Their role-play ended when I was twelve, and their divorce hit me hard.

I remember my father taking us kids to the park to tell us the news. My 13-year-old brother didn't say a thing, and my sister—eleven at the time—only giggled. I, on the other hand, cried like a baby. I was devastated. I couldn't understand why our "normal life" was being destroyed. "This has to be my fault," I thought.

Some time later, my mother married Ron. He and my mom fought constantly, and at times, I thought I'd go crazy. Laying in bed at night, I could distinctly hear the sound of Ron's fist hitting Mom.

The craziness went on for years. Then one day, Ron went totally insane. He battered my mother half to death, then smashed up the furniture, and began burning it in the fireplace. I was down the street at a friend's house. By the time I heard about it, Ron had already been holding a gun on my mother for nearly four hours.

After the police arrived, a single shot rang out. Without thinking, I ran inside where I found Ron lying face up on the living room floor, the rifle still in his hands. He died moments later from a self-inflicted bullet wound.

As the years passed, every day brought new pain, loneliness, and more questions without answers. I wanted to scream out for help, but no one was there to listen. "Why?" I kept asking myself. "What have I done to deserve the life I've had?"

Life had let me down, and I wanted out, so I swallowed a container of codeine tablets. Somehow, I survived, waking up the following afternoon. Life continued to drag on, oblivious to my gesture of defiance.

Larry Shelton, a friend from work, came by to see me several weeks later. He was a very religious guy, always talking about how good Jesus was to him. He'd been after me to come to his house for dinner, and I'd always managed to politely refuse.

I already believed that Jesus was the Son of God, but somehow Larry's life was different. One thing I knew for sure—whatever he had, I wanted some of it. If he'd found answers in his religion, I was willing to let him tell me about it.

After dinner, I began questioning him and his wife about their beliefs. They didn't preach at me or rattle off some mysterious dogma. Instead, from the depths of their hearts, they offered me a new life through Jesus Christ.

I saw what they had wasn't just "a religion," but a deeply personal relationship with God through Jesus Christ. "God is love," Larry told me.

We prayed together, and when we'd finished, I felt as if 1,000 tons had been lifted from my shoulders. I was instantly enveloped in great peace and contentment. I cried from overwhelming happiness—for the first time in my life. I knew that God loved me and cared for me.

Of course, becoming a Christian didn't solve all my problems. Homosexual desires didn't stop overnight—although at first I thought they would. I had not been sexually involved with anyone since my youth, but despite my fasting and prayers, homosexual feelings persisted through college. I kept thinking if maybe I was just a better Christian and believed more in God, I would be "healed."

After leaving college early one semester, I returned home feeling discouraged and disheartened. I felt I had done everything I could to get rid of my homosexual desires, yet they persisted. I met Brian a month later, and we became sexually involved.

Our relationship lasted for about three and a half years. Toward the end of it, I became despondent and suicidal. I wanted a life with God, yet I wanted a life with Brian. The conflict tore me up. In my journal I wrote: "How is it possible to love something so much while hating it even more? I love being loved, feeling loved. I find enormous pleasure in the intimacy we share, in loving and caring for Brian. But something's missing. . . . Why is it that things with Brian were satisfying at first, yet aren't any longer? Now the only satisfaction I find in our relationship occurs while having sex, and even then it doesn't obviate my inner longing for something else. . . .

"I didn't choose to be gay. I hate being different, yet I've never had any say in the matter, so it seems perfectly fitting now—now that I've had more than my fill of all the pressures and fears—to take the one action I can call my own. I just want to be free from this hell I'm living in."

At about this time, I attended a Christian meeting for men seeking to overcome homosexual problems. I was determined not to say
anything at first. Then I told the group where I was coming from,
told them I had a gun to my head, and that if they didn't offer a
viable alternative, I didn't feel there was any alternative except to pull
the trigger.

Well, that night there was a glimmer of hope. It didn't seem like
much at first, but it was enough to keep me going until the group's
next meeting. The first few weeks were a real struggle, but one day I
realized that the more I learned, the less I wanted to die. I immersed
myself in books, seminars, and counseling.

As I applied what I learned, I kept getting stronger and stronger.
With each passing day, I was filled with greater expectations and
dreams for the future. Hope and knowledge took the place of my
fears and doubts. I saw all of life through new eyes; where only darkness had existed before, there was bright, shining light. Within three
and a half months of that first meeting, I broke up with Brian.

It continued to be a struggle. In the beginning I almost always
gave in, although I tried not to and prayed for the strength to resist. I
grew terribly discouraged and thought I'd never succeed in changing.
Then I began analyzing my sexual desires. The key question I asked
was, "How did I feel when I wanted Brian sexually?" The resulting
insight brought me the freedom I was seeking. I had to learn to deal
with the source of my sexual drive, not with my behavior, for I discovered that most of my feelings weren't sexually based at all. I'd just
interpreted them that way, keeping to my old established pattern.

I analyzed how I felt before I slipped up. Sometimes I was
lonely. Other times I felt inadequate. And at times I wanted to be
with Brian just to love and be loved, when I wanted to be intimate
with another human being—normal, valid needs I tried to satisfy in
a homosexual way.

Slowly and gently, God began exposing issues even deeper than
my homosexual feelings. Through prayerful introspection, I was able
to pinpoint the issues, then begin dealing with them one at a time. I
began working through past hurts, misconceptions, and my wrong
responses. I finally took responsibility for my actions. I no longer felt
a helpless victim of past circumstances.

It took me approximately two years to comprehend the root causes of my homosexuality and to completely sever my sexual and emotional ties with Brian. Nearly another year and a half passed before I reached a plateau where I was no longer sexually attracted to men, nor did I yet have any desire for women. It was still another two years before I grew into my true heterosexual identity with its subsequent attractions and desires for the opposite sex.

Unfortunately, my views of women and femininity had been damaged as a child by the pornography my father had in the house. As I grew older, I thought of girls only as sexual objects. Because I already felt inadequate in my masculinity, those feelings frightened me. My sexual feelings for women were blocked because my need for men was so much greater. I had to learn normal, healthy, and proper ways of perceiving and responding to women.

Many of my experiences were beyond my control, but my responses were of my own choosing. A wrong response here, another one there—eventually, they all added up to a distorted image of myself that God didn't intend.

We try to find our way in life around the terrible void that exists in each of us until it's filled by the love of Jesus Christ. Although people try to fill that void in a variety of ways—with sex, power, money, possessions, whatever—so they can cross over, it can't be done. We cannot truly experience contentment and peace until we've welcomed the Savior into our lives. It is Him we must identify with and strive to be like.

(Parts of this story can be found in Jeff Konrad's book, *You Don't Have to Be Gay*, listed in Appendix B.)

MICHELLE

Where did my feelings for women originate? I don't have any idea. I was the youngest of eight children in a very "typical" Mormon family. I was raised in the Church by good parents, and I had about the most normal childhood of anyone I know. I went to Church every Sunday, had lots of friends, got good grades in school, played sports, and loved my family. I felt like any other normal, happy kid. I was always attracted to other girls, and that seemed perfectly normal. I had elementary school crushes on girls and women teachers.

The first time I felt something was abnormal was when I was nine years old. My cousin and I were playing like we were going on a double date. He pretended to have a girlfriend, and I pretended to have a girlfriend. We both pretended to kiss them good night. My mother and older sister came home and asked what we were playing. I told them, and I will never forget the looks on their faces and how uncomfortable the whole situation suddenly felt. What seemed like an innocent expression of my feelings brought shame. That is the one harmful experience of my childhood. I started to believe something was wrong with me, and that I wasn't liked because of it.

I learned to hide my true feelings and began pretending I was whoever I thought people wanted me to be. When I was thirteen, I discovered they had a name for my kind. I was "gay." With that label also came "evil" and "perverted." I didn't feel evil. At least I didn't feel evil up to that point. I loved church and went every Sunday. I loved my family and friends. I always tried very hard to treat others kindly. But the definition of gay fit me, so I decided I must be evil and perverted.

Not long after that is when my suicidal feelings began. It was just so hard to put on a charade all the time. And even worse was the fact that others liked who I pretended to be. I was afraid I would lose them as friends if I told the truth and let them know who I really was. Life is hard enough as a teenager, and living a double life made it harder. It didn't seem to be worth all the effort.

Growing up in the Church, I had heard rude comments about "those people." The most devastating statement I had heard was, "I'd rather my daughter be dead than be a lesbian." That sure made me want to run right out and share my deepest, most honest feelings with people. Actually, I *did* want to open up and trust somebody. I wanted to share my heavy burden, but my fear of being condemned kept me from doing so.

What had I ever done that was so horrible someone would rather I was dead? Just because I had feelings that came as naturally to me as attractions toward the opposite sex came for everyone else. Feelings I had never asked for, feelings I didn't want, feelings that scared me and made me want to hide my face in shame, even though I had never acted on those feelings. What had I done that was so horrible?

It was my own mother who had said that. My mother, who had taught me to follow Christ, had looked me straight in the eye and said, "I'd rather my daughter be dead than be a lesbian."

I wanted to be dead, all right. I'm not sure why I didn't kill myself. I was in high school at the time. I never told my mother about my homosexual feelings. I never would have told anyone. She found out because she read it in my journal; the journal that was my only confidant, the only one who knew everything about me and still accepted me.

In college the conflict became even greater. I stopped going to church. In order to cover up my homosexual feelings or deny them or prove they weren't true, I decided to date guys—a lot of guys. Not only did I date them, I thought that becoming sexually involved with them would prove I was a "heterosexual." And with that label would surely come "normal" and "righteous." My plan backfired. My attraction toward women intensified, and I felt even worse about myself.

I received my associate's degree and transfered to a university that had an organization called the Lesbian and Gay Student Union (LGSU). I could no longer live the lie of going to church and pretending to be just like everyone else. The guilt pangs were too much for me. I decided to give in to the homosexual feelings that had plagued me all those years.

When I attended my first LGSU meeting, I had this incredible sense of belonging. It was at an LGSU meeting that I was introduced to Stacy. She was the first woman I became involved with. The most compelling aspect of our relationship was not the physical part. It was the emotional part. The relationship was caring, and we were best friends. I was loved for who I was. I finally felt free. I wanted to shout at the top of my lungs, "I'm gay, and I'm happy about it!"

My whole life began to revolve around the gay lifestyle. All my friends were gay and every social event I attended was with my gay friends. I couldn't believe I was with so many people who loved and accepted me and felt the same way I did.

After I broke up with Stacy, I met Angie. I was sure she was "the one." She had also grown up in a large Mormon family and had a strong religious background. We had so many things in common. She'd felt the same rejection and confusion about the Church. We both believed in Christ and the Book of Mormon, so we'd study the scriptures and pray together. The relationship felt right. We were convinced it was ordained of God and that soon the Church would receive the answer to the question that no one had bothered to ask yet. "Did God approve of homosexual marriages?" Of course He did. We thought for sure we had already received our answer from God. Certainly the Brethren would, too.

Angie and I lived together for several years. Occasionally I would question whether or not it was really as right as I thought it was. Then, I began to feel like it was wrong. The Spirit was working on me. I finally decided to talk to a good friend and to a bishop for advice. Each time, after talking to one of them, I would try to follow their counsel and leave Angie. I'd go away for a while but couldn't handle being alone. I kept leaving and returning. What I thought was freedom, a homosexual relationship, was really more like a prison, and I couldn't escape.

I gave up hope of finding happiness. I figured I was destined to live in silent misery as some sort of punishment for not living God's commandments. I deserved to be miserable. I was in despair and crying all the time. I saw suicide as the only way out.

At this point a miracle occurred. Laura, a friend I had grown up with, called me. She said she felt strongly impressed that I needed to talk with someone. All it took was one person following the Spirit and expressing Christlike love to keep me from taking my own life. After hearing of my situation and feeling my pain, she told me I needed to make a clean break from Angie and everyone else. She invited me to live with her in a different city. If I wanted to get out I knew I would have to leave anything and everything that even remotely reminded me of the gay lifestyle. I knew that was what the Lord required. I needed to sacrifice everything to show Him I was willing to let Him captain my life.

It wasn't an easy decision. I had to quit my job, leave my relationship and all of my friends, and move to another city. But I knew it was right, so I did. Laura was a good influence on me. She told me that two things would change my life—the Book of Mormon and fervent prayer. I had done those things before, but this time was different. Those two things, along with Laura's faith-filled friendship, brought me to a knowledge of the power of God and helped me build a personal relationship with my Lord and Savior, Jesus Christ.

It is Jesus Christ who has enabled me to completely leave homosexuality behind. Getting back into the scriptures was difficult because for a long time I had only applied the easy ones and had twisted the others so they'd fit in with my lifestyle. Once I became humble, submissive, and spiritual rather than carnal and natural, my desires really began to change. It was slow at first, but the more I surrounded myself with the right people, places, and thoughts, the more I *desired* to be surrounded by them.

The Lord changed my heart, my whole being, once I did everything I could to take myself out of the wrong situations. The void in my life became filled with His goodness, and that is when I really began to feel the change. It wasn't any one particular moment. It was, and still is, a process—a process of becoming more and more like my Savior.

I will never return to homosexual relationships. With Christ there is peace. I will not, I cannot, lose that constant companionship of the Lord's Spirit, for it is my life. Without Him I have no life.

Lydia

The school specialist labeled me a "troubled child" the first week of kindergarten. Many physical and mental tests were taken. This pattern would follow me into junior high. Each year I struggled a little more scholastically but went way off the charts in emotional disorders. I had been adopted, and my adoption became an issue of abandonment and resentment. I remember a card I received from my grandpa. In it he wrote, "You are another little girl whom no one wanted. We are grateful your mom and dad took you in."

I also remember some fun things we did as a family. We had great family home evenings. Both of my parents sacrificed for me.

I'm not sure what caused the explosion in my heart or my spirit, but by age ten I was close to being totally out of control. I began stealing and lying. I felt angry, resentful, and overwhelmingly lonely. I was really mad at my siblings most of the time. They excluded me from everything. My dad and I were close, but I often fought with my mom. All my bad habits just kept getting bigger as did my fears and the all-encompassing loneliness.

School got worse. Church got worse. And home got much worse. I'd thought of running away several times. Finally, one day I said to my dad that I was either going to destroy myself or the whole family. I wanted to leave as soon as possible. By this point my parents were so tired, they consented. I was moved into Social Services through the Church, but they, in turn, had to hand me over to the court system.

In the years that followed, I was moved around to several different group homes. I stayed in school and remained isolated. My five other roomies at the home were also very hard core. For once in my life I was not the worst kid. But my feelings and conscience were so layered with anger it didn't seem to matter.

Trudy, my roommate at the girls home, was the first person I felt real love and compassion for. She was the first human (other than my dad) who could touch me without making me feel scared or want to run. A flicker of love emerged through my hardened shell. But after being with her for four months, she was arrested.

I actually graduated from high school and moved into my own little place, near a gay bar. I'd hang out there during the week and on weekends, then go to church on Sunday. Deep inside, I still believed the gospel was true, but I felt so confused. Why did it hurt—physically and spiritually—to go to Heavenly Father's house? The harder it was to be at church, the easier it was to go to socials, bars, meetings, and pow-wows with my new "family." I wanted to be liked.

Later, I quit going to church and decided to express myself with my body. I shaved off part of my hair and colored the rest of it—pink to green to black—depending on my mood. I got my nose pierced. I figured sin wasn't sin until someone saw it. I floundered—becoming hardened, resentful, and scared.

You can never get enough of what you don't really need but think you want. My body seemed to crave physical contact. I tried to cure the loneliness with sexual relationships with women. Satan presented a distorted love which seemed better than no love at all.

Sex began to fill my life. I had no conscience. The Spirit left me. I was absolutely determined to fill the crater in my heart. I was sure sex was the answer.

There were times my body screamed for a gentle touch—not a sexual touch, just gentle contact. I was convinced that I would be abandoned. I decided to try to get all I could, while I still could. I tried to pacify, if even for a small moment, the consuming loneliness my spirit and body felt.

Sometimes I would stop acting out sexually for a few days, but each time I would fall back in. When I tried to pull away there would be days with no human contact, not even shaking hands. My body kept screaming at me, demanding to be touched. Sexual addiction engulfed me.

It was at this point in my life that my supervisor at work, Susan, somehow saw through my shell to the flicker of light within. She was determined to make me see it. She didn't move in too fast but quickly enough to show me she wasn't scared of me. She and her husband, Ken, were Church members who'd had many experiences with the spiritually impaired. We spent a lot of time just hanging out—movies, rides, and long walks. I really looked forward to being with them. I began to feel things that I didn't want to count on, like happiness and safety.

With the exception of the stability offered by Susan and Ken, life was an emotional roller coaster. I hated my work, myself, and God. As if things weren't bad enough, my dad died. I lost the only person in my family who had offered me complete love and acceptance.

I went to gay bars during the week and on Saturday nights, and started going to church on Sunday. One day I was called in by the bishop to have a chat. Someone had reported me, and a Church disciplinary council was held. The only thing I knew was that I wanted to see my dad again. I knew it would take a miracle to clean up my life and with him on the other side of the veil, maybe that could happen. I knew I had to go all the way out of the Church before I could come back in. My request was to be excommunicated and they agreed.

As Susan and I left the disciplinary council that night, I had found hope for change. It was such a relief. Now it was time for the mighty change promised to me in the Book of Mormon. I knew my life would push that promise to its limits.

Being outside of baptism is a dangerous place to be during the last days. However, I received help from above. Deep down inside, under all the hate and fear, I always knew Jesus was the Christ. I knew He had suffered in Gethsemane for me. He gave this gift to me freely, for which I owed Him love and devotion.

I moved into a new ward and met with a bishop who became a key player in my spiritual overhaul. Repenting became an 80-hour-a-week job. People asked me what I did for a living, and quite bluntly I would reply, "Repent. And you?" I gave up many physical possessions and cut off all contact with old girlfriends. I never felt so alone in my life. The purging of my spirit was so overwhelming at times that I thought I was trying the impossible. But the bishop had promised me he would believe in me enough for both of us until I could reclaim my heart.

When the Church disciplinary council was reconvened, the Lord, through the bishop, declared that I was ready to be rebaptized. There was a beautiful spirit at my baptism. The room was filled to capacity and so was my heart. I was overwhelmed. My bishop spoke of my achievements and the monumental changes he had seen in my life.

Things have been difficult, but the peace I feel today is something I never thought I could feel. I had to be willing to give up everything—pride, resentment, fear and confusion, and women. As I did, I was blessed with the comfort of the Comforter. I have finally found dry land after years of searching through stormy seas.

Do I still get lonely? With the Holy Ghost I am never alone as long as I remain worthy. When I partake of the sacrament, I not only feel a spiritual and emotional fulfillment, but also a physical one. And I'm finding I'm not such bad company after all. I continue to pray for my "best friend," hoping that he is doing all that is required of him so that we will both be ready when the time comes for us to meet.

Do I still struggle with homosexual desires? Once in a while I feel very lonely physically, and I don't mean sexually. I miss those relationships with women sometimes, but I will not sacrifice the companionship of the Holy Ghost for anything on this planet. I ask myself which I want more, and the Comforter always prevails. I remember to give thanks for the boundaries I used to curse as I now understand they are there to protect me, not trap me.

I will go through the temple soon. For each promise I make, there will be a greater promise made to me. Growing up, I wasn't allowed a key to my house. Soon I will receive the key to eternal life as I go through the temple.

TONY

My name is Tony. I'm thirty-four years old, and I have questioned my sexual identity ever since I was a young boy. I remember thinking as a small child that God had made a mistake. I knew that I would have made a better girl than boy. I even told my friends that I wished I was half boy and half girl. The girl part for my sake and the boy to please everyone else.

I always felt uncomfortable around other boys when they were doing boy things like baseball or basketball. I was never involved with my father in sports and never learned to play, so I was horrible at it. I'd get made fun of and that was painful. Soon I avoided sports altogether.

I was very soft hearted and always felt sorry for other people. Growing up I had learned to please people in an effort to maintain peace. At home I took it upon myself to lessen the contention. I was always bothered that no one in my family seemed to like each other. I tried hard to be the perfect child. I never gave my parents any problems, and they never worried about me.

I started acting out sexually with another boy before I had even started puberty. I always thought that was the reason I felt gay. I continued indulging sexually until I was seventeen years old. Then I told my bishop. I had remembered hearing all these talks on how a burden would be lifted once a person had confessed. But after talking to the bishop, I felt rotten. I felt so ashamed, even though the bishop didn't act too concerned. I had gone to him hoping for some answers, and I left feeling like I had simply met some standard requirement for repentance.

I read all the pamphlets on homosexuality and other talks given by general authorities. I learned that if I kept the commandments, Christ would heal me. So I put a lid on my feelings and decided to go on a mission. After I returned from serving a faithful mission, I joined the army. Later I decided it was time to get married. I figured marriage would give me the opportunity to undo the "deviant" behavior I had gotten myself into so early in life.

Luckily for me, I married a wonderful woman. I decided not to tell her about my issue because I was sure that it would no longer be a problem. After all, I had not acted out homosexually since I was seventeen and now I was twenty-three. Before I had even been married twenty-four hours, I began to feel like I had made a big mistake. I could function fine sexually but I felt rotten inside, like I was living a big lie. Years earlier I'd had nightmares about being married, and now I felt like I was living those nightmares and couldn't wake up.

On my honeymoon I got so depressed I started to cry. Why couldn't I be like other guys? This was the time in life everyone lived for, sharing something intimate with a beautiful woman. My poor wife saw me crying and asked what was wrong. All I could say was that something was bothering me and that I would never tell her. I needed help so badly. I thought, I have to tell my dad. He'll help me.

As soon as we got home from our honeymoon I went to see my parents. I told my father how I'd felt for twenty years and what I'd kept inside. He said that I had always been his "third daughter," and he laughed a little bit. My father never was one for being very sensitive to someone's feelings. I was being shredded from the inside out, and it bugged me that he wasn't taking it seriously. I said "Dad, I don't know what to do." He wanted to help, but he didn't know what to do either.

As married life began, I knew I couldn't live that way very long. I called LDS Social Services to see if they could help. They wouldn't see me without my bishop's recommendation. I didn't want to go to my bishop because I didn't have any "unresolved sins" to take care of, and the whole thing was too painful for me to talk about.

I decided a year would be ample time for me to grow into "heterosexuality." Four months into our marriage my wife got pregnant.

Then I felt like it was no longer an option for me to get out in a year. I put the lid on it again, and I adjusted to married life. I read books on positive thinking, and they really helped me through a series of depressions. Depression became a way of life for me.

About four years into our marriage, I met this really nice guy named Bill. We had so much in common. We were both married, and our kids were about the same age. Three weeks into our friendship, Bill told me he felt trapped in a gay world. I welcomed the opportunity to tell him about my own life.

My feelings for Bill soon grew. I remember thinking, "I deserve this." After all, hadn't I kept the commandments and tried to relearn sexual behavior? I fought the feeling of wanting to be with him sexually. Why hadn't I felt this kind of desire for my wife on my honeymoon?

I became more and more confused. Bill and I were spending as much time together as possible. I was meeting him for lunch, after work, and any time I could make an excuse to sneak away. We double dated with our wives. It was wild. As long as I was with him I felt secure. When I wasn't with him, I was depressed and longed to talk to him or be with him. I was very unstable.

My wife became jealous of the time that Bill and I were spending together. I was finding it difficult to juggle time, family, Bill, and my emotions. During all this I'd resisted becoming sexually involved, but I knew I was getting close and had already crossed certain lines, which made me feel ashamed.

I knew I had to end the friendship. We'd become too dependent on each other, and I didn't feel good about what we were doing to our families. We were both having a difficult time with things, so we made the decision to stop seeing each other.

I sulked for months afterward and wondered what to do. I felt like I was messing up my life and the life of my family. I finally went and talked to my bishop about it and was able to unload. Unlike the first time, when I was a teenager, it felt good to be able to admit and accept where I was in life and say I didn't know what to do. It seemed that as much as I had tried, I hadn't been able to control my desires. Opening up to the bishop was cleansing. He was very supportive and understanding. I'd hit close to home for him because he had a brother who was living a gay lifestyle. I felt nothing but love and concern from the bishop, even though he didn't have any answers.

My wife still didn't know. I knew she was in love with the person she thought I was. I had to tell her. It was one of the hardest things I've ever done. When I told her, she said she'd give it a year.

I began one-on-one therapy which was a waste of money and time. The therapist couldn't "figure me out," and I started playing the role of pleaser again. I also became involved with group therapy. It was great to talk to people about feelings and remove a lot of the isolation. It was liberating. I started playing basketball with the group. I loved being with my friends who understood me and accepted me. I developed skills I never knew I had and started to feel a change inside. I remember feeling that the interaction with those guys was more profound and meaningful than any sexual experience I'd had with another guy.

I was involved with the support group and sports program for about a year and a half. In the beginning, I lived for the opportunity to be with those guys in group. I didn't think I'd tire of it, but I started to grow out of the need for that intense interaction.

I branched out just a little bit and shared my feelings with a couple of friends and experienced unconditional love. I'd always thought it would bother people. Even though they were concerned for me, they still told me they loved me and that it didn't matter.

I read that homosexual desires grow out of an unmet need to be legitimately loved by someone of the same sex and that those needs can be met in appropriate ways. That sounded so beautiful to me. Deep down inside, all I ever wanted was to be loved.

I found that being totally honest with myself was the only way to find peace. I don't confess to being "cured," whatever that means. I do say I'm no longer depressed. I understand myself, and I don't feel so confused. I feel very happy with who I am. I know I have needs like everyone. I need to love, be loved, and to have true friends in my life. Now I let people in, and it's great.

When I was first married, I thought marriage and family life were going to pull me apart. Looking back, I see that my wife and children have helped pull me together. My relationship with my wife is wonderful now. I feel like we're a team and there are no gulfs between us. Even though we've traveled a rough road, we're closer and more understanding of each other because of it.

Once I felt plagued by homosexual feelings. Now I occasionally have some feelings, which signal to me that some needs still must be met. I haven't always been able to say this, but I love myself. That alone has created so much healing. I have realized my own worth. I've been taught I am a valuable person. Now I know I am a whole, courageous, loving man.

JENNIFER

I first heard about the Mormon church when I was in high school. At that time, I was more than a little confused. I was a mess. My father was an alcoholic. In fact, I really don't remember him being sober. I never talked to either one of my parents very much.

I always felt different growing up. I really just wanted to be good—to do what was right—whatever that was. I was never taught. I tried to teach myself. I thought I was a failure, a nobody. Drinking provided temporary relief. No one else was there to share the pain.

I didn't like guys, but I dated a few. They got what they wanted—sex. I had to be drunk first. They scared me. Sometimes men still scare me. Throughout my life men had always done things to me I didn't want them to do.

I became very confused. I couldn't tell what was bad and what was good. My father said my feelings were bad and wrong. So I quit feeling. He was my father. Father knows best.

I had always liked women because they didn't hurt me. I remember playing house in the 6th grade with a girlfriend of mine. I would be the husband and she would be the wife. We would hug and kiss and that seemed perfectly normal.

During high school I had this crush on an older girl. I fantasized about her a lot, but never told her about my feelings.

I went to college and kept drinking frequently. I'd lock the door to my room and cry uncontrollably for no reason. I just knew I hurt inside. I dropped out of my last year of college because of finances and moved in with my aunt. It was then that I met Karen who was a Mormon. We became physically involved and soon moved in together.

Strangely enough, I went to church with Karen. I began taking the discussions and was baptized, even though we were still physically involved. I lied in the interview. I lied to God. My baptism wasn't even right. Couldn't I do anything right? I truly did believe in the gospel. Something deep inside knew it was true. And the two principles that impressed me the most were the law of chastity and the Word of Wisdom.

After five years of living with Karen, I noticed that a part of me was screaming for help. I finally listened to the cry and confessed to my bishop, so I could put my life in order. I repented and made progress. The bishop then invited me to serve a mini-mission. I shared with him my desire to go on a full-time mission. He consented. I will never forget the process. I needed to talk to the stake president who informed me that I would need to meet with a General Authority. I was scared. The next thing I knew I was flying to Salt Lake to meet with a General Authority. He was a kind man. He asked me about myself, my interests, my family, and my desire to serve a mission. He declared that I was worthy to go. I was so excited.

I served a faithful mission, and it was a wonderful experience. I returned on a spiritual high. Then, the darkness and the turmoil and the fear returned. I didn't want to do anything. I stayed in my room. I felt like nothing. Where was God? Where was the comfort I so desired? What was wrong with me?

I moved and got a new job, and life started looking up. Then Julie came into my life. I fell in love with her. We became involved emotionally and physically. My pain left. I felt comfort, love, acceptance, and fulfillment. Yet, as time went on, I had to ask myself, if I have found all of these things, why does there seem to be a conflict? Deep inside I knew the answer. It was a voice telling me that what I was doing was not right. I had stopped wearing my garments because I didn't want to defile something sacred. Really, I knew I was still defiling something just as sacred, myself.

But I had finally found a way to rid myself of fear and pain. I had safety and comfort. There would never be comfort in a relationship with a man. I hurt too much. I lost who I was. I couldn't even remember who I was. I had lost my identity. I guess that's when I decided I wanted to be a boy so I could treat women the way they should be treated.

Over time, there still was no peace, no matter how Julie made me feel. Finally, we both went in to see a bishop. I was put on probation, with one of the requirements being that I stop seeing Julie. Unfortunately, I couldn't prevent myself, no matter how hard I tried.

Once again I confessed to the bishop, and he decided a disciplinary council should be held. I wanted to get back fully into the Church. I worked so hard and it hurt so bad. I started to pray every day and read my scriptures. I attended all my meetings. I met several friends who were Church members. Kerry was probably the biggest help. I talked to her almost every day on the phone. She would encourage me and bear her testimony of the Savior. She'd had lots of problems and with the help of the Savior, she had been healed. I could feel her Spirit, and her example was good for me to see.

I opened my heart to my bishop and, in turn, he began to open his heart to me and receive understanding. We began to work together. Our relationship started out rocky, but it got much better. I know the Spirit helped.

I stayed away from Julie and continued to grow closer to the Spirit. The time came when I was taken off probation. My only question was, "When can I go back to the temple?" "Now" was his reply. It was amazing to me. Even in the temple, my deep pain remained. But I got a glimpse of what the celestial kingdom would be like when I was greeted by my friends in the celestial room.

The battle continued to be very difficult. What I loved, was being taken away. I was very angry. I was even angry at Heavenly Father because I wanted to be good and happy but I didn't find those feelings at church. Why? Where was it? Why couldn't I find it?

I began seeing a counselor. She had dealt with people struggling with homosexual desires before. She helped me learn and grow and understand myself. For so many years I had thought I was bad. I could hear the words that my father had taught me to believe: "You're a bad, bad girl." I was bad. I had always wanted to be good, but I was bad.

I looked forward to counseling sessions until they became frightening. We discussed what I had a sense of, but kept denying; perhaps my father had molested me. The thoughts and memories
started to come up, and I kept forcing them back down. I would get
so scared I couldn't even talk. I refused to believe it had happened. I
guess I had blocked it out because that was the only way I could deal
with it. Now it all seemed like a bad dream or something. In fact, I
would have nightmares about my father. I got to where I would
hardly sleep at all because I didn't want to dream.

I wanted to feel better. I could not have the comfort of a woman,
which made it feel like I could not have any comfort at all. "I want
FREEDOM. I want FREEDOM from memories of my father and
from fearing men because of what they might do to me. I want
FREEDOM from the old Jennifer who learned to do what she did in
her life so she could survive. I want FREEDOM from homosexuality!"

One night I watched a movie about a girl who tried to tell
people she had been sexually abused by her father, but no one believed her. Then it hit me. I was faced with the vivid, conscious
memory that my father truly had molested me. It was more real than
ever before. I remembered being abused by my father and then him
telling me that no one would believe me if I told them what happened.

"No one would believe me!" There was no way out of my trap. It
seemed to be happening to me all over again, right at that moment.
It was like I could hear my father's footsteps coming up the stairs and
I knew he was going to get me. It was so real. The fear I kept hidden
came out and choked me. There was no way to get away from him.
Or was there?

I went into the bathroom, tore apart a razor blade and slit my
wrist. In that horrifying moment I realized that slitting my wrist was
less painful than the pain I had felt inside all those years. Before I
could finish myself off, a friend came in, and my life was spared.

I talked to my friend Kerry that night, and one of many miracles
happened. She believed me when I told her about my father. Then
the whole room got lighter, and I felt like Christ was taking my hand.
I was safe, for the first time in my life. I felt the Savior's love. I found

out how real Jesus Christ can be. He understands more than I thought. I discovered that He was and is very aware of me.

Heavenly Father, Jesus Christ, friends, and a caring counselor have helped me become free from abuse and homosexual attractions. Before, my heart was too fearful to open up and stand up for what it believed. My father stole my heart from me. A heart that had self-worth. A heart that knew she was a daughter of God. A heart that trusted in God to protect her. My heart had become layered with hate, anger, fear, betrayal, loss of identity, and lack of trust in any-one.

Now my heart is finding freedom. Things I never thought could change, are changing. I'm starting to like myself and see that I'm not bad. I even had a date with a man and thought he was kind and caring. I am finding out who I am. When I shut down on all those bad things, I also shut down on all the good parts of me.

This journey has been horrible. There were times when I wondered if I would ever see the light. I testify that the light is there, just beyond the darkness. Continuing obedience and sacrifice have gotten me through the darkness. It's not easy, but, then, neither was Christ's journey.

Miracles have not ceased. Heavenly Father and Jesus Christ are real. They are waiting for us to take their hand so, together, we can overcome. I promise with all my heart, in the name of Jesus Christ, that change is possible.

Appendix B

AMCAP (Association of Mormon Counselors and Psychotherapists) *Journal*, vol. 19, no. 1 (1993). Available through Evergreen or AMCAP, 2500 E. 1700 South, Salt Lake City, Ut. 84108. An excellent collection of articles discussing homosexuality from an LDS viewpoint. Helpful for men and women seeking freedom from same-sex attraction, as well as for counselors and leaders.

John and Martha Nibley Beck. *Breaking the Cycle of Compulsive Behavior.* Salt Lake City: Deseret Book Co., 1990. Helpful for men and women seeking freedom from same-sex attraction, especially when compulsive behavior is involved.

Darlene Bogle. *Long Road to Love.* Old Tappan, N. J.: Chosen Books, 1985. The personal account of one Christian woman's journey out of lesbianism. Helpful for women who seek freedom from same-sex attraction.

Darlene Bogle. *Strangers in a Christian Land.* Old Tappan, N. J.: Chosen Books, 1990. For all who struggle with same-sex attraction and for those who seek to help.

William Byne and Bruce Parsons. "Human Sexual Orientation: The Biologic Theories Reappraised." *Archive of General Psychiatry,* vol. 50 (Mar. 1993):228-38. A technical, critical review presenting evidence that a biologic theory is lacking.

Patrick Carnes. *Don't Call It Love: Recovery from Sexual Addiction.* New York: Bantam Books, 1991. Helpful for all who struggle with sexual addictions.

William Consiglio. *Homosexual No More.* Wheaton, Ill.: Victor Books, 1991. Primarily for men seeking freedom from same-sex attraction.

Joe Dallas. *Desires in Conflict: Answering the Struggle for Sexual Identity.* Eugene, Oreg.: Harvest House, 1991. Written by a Christian who has overcome. An excellent resource for men and women seeking freedom from same-sex attraction and those who wish to help them.

Richard Friedman and Jennifer Downey, "Neurobiology and Sexual Orientation: Current Relationships." *Journal of Neuropsychiatry and Clinical Neurosciences,* vol. 5, no. 2 (Spring 1993):131–153. Discusses the complex issue of human sexual orientation, emphasizing the biopsychosocial model.

Jeanette Howard. *Out of Egypt: Leaving Lesbianism Behind.* London: Monarch Publishing, 1991. One Christian's journey out of lesbianism. Some of the Christian philosophy is not consistent with the LDS perspective.

Barbara Johnson. *Fresh Elastic for Stretched-Out Moms.* Old Tappan, N. J.: Fleming H. Revell Co., 1986. Helpful for loved ones.

Barbara Johnson. *Where Does a Mother Go to Resign?* Minneapolis: Bethany House, 1979. A witty and sympathetic look into the struggles of a parent. Helpful for parents.

Jeff Konrad. *You Don't Have to Be Gay: Hope and Freedom for Males Struggling with Homosexuality or for Those Who Know of Someone Who Is.* Newport Beach, Calif.: Pacific Publishing, 1987. Using a series of letters, this book tells Jeff's personal account of overcoming same-sex attraction. Helpful for men.

Elisabeth Kübler-Ross. *AIDS: The Ultimate Challenge.* New York: Macmillan, 1987.

Elizabeth R. Moberly. *Homosexuality: A New Christian Ethic.* Greenwood S.C.: Attic Press, 1983. A rather technical book discussing same-sex needs and homosexuality. Can be helpful for men and women.

Betty Clare Moffatt. *When Someone You Love Has AIDS.* New York, N.Y.: Nal/Dutton Press, 1986.

Joseph Nicolosi. *Healing Homosexuality: Case Stories in Reparative Therapy.* North Vale, N. J.: Jason Aaronson, 1993. Helpful for men and counselors.

Joseph Nicolosi. *Reparative Therapy of Male Homosexuality: A New Clinical Approach.* North Vale, N. J.: Jason Aaronson, 1991. A scholarly book helpful for men, although some may not fit the developmental pattern presented.

Judith A. Reisman and Edward W. Eichel. *Kinsey, Sex, and Fraud: The Indoctrination of a People.* New York, N.Y.: Huntington House, 1990.

G. A. Rekers. *Growing Up Straight: What Families Should Know about Homosexuality.* Chicago, Ill.: Moody Press, 1982.

Lori Thorkelson Rentzel. *Emotional Dependency.* San Rafael, Calif.: Exodus International, 1984. A pamphlet especially helpful for women.

Elaine V. Siegel. *Female Homosexuality: Choice without Volition.* Hillsdale, N. J.: Analytic Press, 1988. A psychoanalytic approach to helping women change sexual orientation.

Charles W. Socarides and Vamik D. Volkan, ed. *Homosexualities and the Therapeutic Process.* Madison, Conn.: International Universities Press, 1991. Very psychoanalytic approach. Helpful mostly for professional counselors.

Gerald J. M. Van den Aardweg. *Homosexuality and Hope.* Ann Arbor, Mich.: Servant Books, 1985. A psychologist's approach to overcoming same-sex attraction with emphasis on self-pity and feelings of inferiority as root causes. Helpful for some men.

Frank Worthen. *Steps Out of Homosexuality.* San Rafael, Calif.: Love in Action, 1984. Written by a Christian who has left homosexuality. More helpful for men.

J. Isamu Yamamoto, ed. *The Crisis of Homosexuality.* Wheaton, Ill.: Victor Books, 1990. An overview of male and female homosexuality, related problems, and what Christian churches can do to help.

ORGANIZATIONS

Evergreen Foundation
    P.O. Box 3
    Salt Lake City, Utah 84110
    Phone: 1-801-535-1658

Offers support groups based on LDS values, in various locations. Currently available for men, with plans to start groups for women. Participants are interviewed before attending group. Friends of Evergreen is a support group for friends and family. Many of the books listed above are available through Evergreen.

Exodus International
    P.O. Box 2121
    San Rafael, California 94912
    Phone: 1-415-454-1017

More than ninety Christian ministries worldwide are Exodus members. Cassette tapes, pamphlets, and videotapes are available for those seeking to overcome same-sex attraction. Also helpful for family, friends, church leaders, and counselors. Materials take a Christian approach to the topic.

Homosexuals Anonymous
    P.O. Box 7881
    Reading, Pennsylvania 19508
    Phone: 1-215-376-1146

A nationwide Christian support group with various materials and a fourteen-step program to help those who seek freedom from same-sex attraction.

Regeneration Books
 P.O. Box 9830
 Baltimore, Maryland 21284-9830

Mail-order resource for Christian books dealing with homosexuality and related topics. Helpful for men and women, counselors, leaders, and family members. Many of the books listed above are available through Regeneration Books.